ZEN ECHOES

Zen Echoes

Classic Kōans with Verse Commentaries by Three Female Chan Masters

Translated and Introduced by
Beata Grant

Foreword by
Susan Moon

Wisdom Publications
199 Elm Street
Somerville, MA 02144 USA
wisdompubs.org

Library of Congress Cataloging-in-Publication Data
Names: Zishou Miaozong, 1095–1170, writer of added commentary. | Grant, Beata, 1954– editor,
    translator.
Title: Zen echoes: classic Koans with verse commentaries by three female Chan masters / trans-
    lated and introduced by Beata Grant; foreword by Susan Moon.
Other titles: Song gu he xiang ji. English | Classic Koans with verse commentaries by three
    female Chan masters
Description: Somerville, MA: Wisdom Publications, [2016] | Includes bibliographical references.
Identifiers: LCCN 2016031575 | ISBN 9781614291879 (pbk.: alk. paper) | ISBN 161429187X (pbk.:
    alk. paper) | ISBN 9781614293712 (ebook)
Subjects: LCSH: Koan.
Classification: LCC BQ9289 .S6613 2016 | DDC 294.3/4432—dc23
LC record available at https://lccn.loc.gov/2016031575

ISBN 978-1-61429-187-9   ebook ISBN 978-1-61429-204-3

21 20 19 18 17
5 4 3 2 1

The image on the cover and title page is a rare woodblock portrait (artist unknown) of a
sevententh-century-woman Chan master by the name of Yikui Chaochen 一揆超琛. This
image appears on the first page of her collection of discourse records, Cantong Yikui Chaochen
chanshi yulu, reprinted in the Jiaxing Dazangjing (Jiaxing Buddhist Canon). 40 Volumes. (Taipei: Xinwenfeng chubanshe, 1987) vol. 39, p. 7.

Cover design by Phil Pascuzzo. Interior design by Gopa & Ted2, Inc. Set in Minion Pro 10.5/15.

Please visit fscus.org.

Table of Contents

Foreword by Susan Moon

In the following pages, you get to hear a conversation between four wise Buddhist women: Miaozong, Baochi, Zukui and their translator, Beata Grant herself. They meet each other right here, across vast distances of time and space, and you get to meet them, too, and hear their interweaving voices.

This is the first English translation of a remarkable book. In the twelfth century, the female Chan master Miaozong wrote commentaries in verse for a number of classic Chan kōans. Five centuries later, two more female masters, Baochi and Zukui, who were friends, added another layer when they collaborated to write verse commentaries in response to Miaozong's verses, as well as to the kōans themselves. In her substantial and informative introduction, Grant speaks of the significance of this book as the first collection of commentaries that is only by women. She provides historical and cultural context for the kōans and verse commentaries, and biographical background on the three women.

How grateful I am to Beata Grant for bringing us these verses. This book reminds me how much we contemporary American Buddhist practitioners and readers of Buddhist literature owe to the scholars. We can't take Beata Grant for granted. Bringing these verses into modern English requires translation beyond translation. It can only be done by a very knowledgeable scholar.

To *translate* means to "carry across," and translating ancient Chinese into modern English takes a lot of carrying, across culture, space, and time: from Chinese characters to the roman alphabet, from China across the Pacific to the West, and in this case from twelfth- and seventeenth-century writers to twenty-first-century readers.

The Chinese characters are printed in the book immediately following the English translation of each kōan and verse. To my eye this delicate code is completely mysterious, and it seems magic that anyone would be able to turn these latticework tiles into English sentences.

As I understand it, a Chinese character contains many possibilities, and sometimes simultaneous meanings and puns. One character can contain many words and can be unpacked in different ways. There are also many cultural and Buddhist references embedded in Chinese writing, so Grant needs to know not just the individual characters, but how they work together in their own cultural context.

Grant must also choose the English idiom that best expresses to us the voices of these long-gone Chinese women. Chan masters, including these three, often spoke bluntly: "It's all a bunch of crap." The imagery is strong: "The nostrils his mother gave him turn black with frostbite." Often surprising: "The white sun in the blue sky grabs the fire and runs off with it." And occasionally gentle: "On the limitless misty waves, a leaf of a boat."

It must be a challenge to ring these changes in English. A few times a footnote says, with disarming transparency, "This translation is tentative," affirming the difficulty of the job. But mostly the footnotes give important and clarifying background information, elucidating many of the references. They are further evidence of Grant's scholarship and are full of wonderful tidbits and stories. Taken by themselves, they could make a lively prose-poem chapbook.

Kōans are famously difficult to "understand" in our ordinary way of thinking, and the verse commentaries hardly straighten things out for us. Chan is nonlinear, and the point is to stretch and open wide the mind, taking us beyond habitual thinking.

So, let the mystery itself be part of the pleasure of the reading. Here is Zukui, responding to the well-known kōan "Nanquan Kills the Cat":

> Below the sharp sword, both were good at turning the body;
> There is nobody walking under the moon along the old road.
> That which was blocked has been transmitted and flourishes;
> At the golden gates, the secret armies halt by imperial decree!

Kōans and commentaries can be read like dreams, like poetry. And these commentaries *are* poetry—after all, they are in verse. They add further chords and resonances to the kōans, as you might expect from the title *The Concordant Sounds Collection of Verse Commentaries.*

Repetition is one way to approach the mystery. I like to memorize a verse that touches me, and say it over and over to myself, until I connect with it like a familiar dream. I chose this verse of Baochi's:

> A mud Buddha does not pass through water;
> Thoroughly merged, nothing left incomplete.
> If you wash with water your face will shine;
> If you drink your tea, your lips will be moist.

I'm drinking my tea right now, and my lips are completely moist. The mud I'm made of is completely dissolved in the watery air.

Once in a while a verse comes along like a simple song, and this welcome, too. Here is Baochi's verse on the kōan "Every Day Is a Good Day":

> On clear days, the sun comes out;
> When it rains, the earth is damp.
> There is no need to think about anything else,
> Except to finish up your business.

One of the things I appreciate about these verses is the open expression of emotion they sometimes contain. (I can't help wondering if this has anything to do with the fact that they are by women.) For example, in response to the kōan about Huike cutting off his arm in order to prove his sincerity to Bodhidharma, Zukui writes,

> He was able to get his mind pacified, but his wrist was severed.
> Thinking about it makes one want to cry out to the high heavens.

And Baochi, commenting on Zhaozhou's challenging question: "Do you have it? Do you have it?" writes, "My breast surges with hot blood; can anyone understand this?"

These verses use words to speak of what is often spoken of in Zen/Chan: the impossibility of expressing the ultimate truth in words. Miaozong says,

To go on and talk about the real Buddha being within
Does nothing but show you're already muddleheaded.

Baochi puts it this way:

The real Buddha sits within.
By putting it into words you've made a mistake—

And yet, here are all these wonderful verses. Thank you, Beata Grant, for making the mistake of putting them into English words.

Introduction

This is a translation of a work that in Chinese is titled *Songgu hexiang ji* 頌古合響集 or *The Concordant Sounds Collection of Verse Commentaries*. Verse commentaries, or *songgu* 頌古, are poems inspired by stories or kōans about buddhas, bodhisattvas, and above all, the great Chan (Zen) masters of the classical period. They were composed primarily by Chan masters, the vast majority of whom historically have been male. The verses in this collection, however, are unique in that they were composed by three female Chan masters, Chan master Miaozong 妙總 from the twelfth century and Chan Masters Baochi 寶持 and Zukui 祖揆 from the seventeenth.

Miaozong (1095–1170) is famous for being one of the first officially recognized female Chan masters in Chinese history. She was also known for her literary talents as well as her religious achievements, and although much of her writing has been lost, many of her verse commentaries were preserved in a fourteenth-century anthology of such verses. Over five hundred years after Miaozong's death, the two Dharma companions Baochi and Zukui were so inspired by these verses that they each composed their own verse commentaries on the same kōans originally commented upon by Miaozong.[1] These kōans, together with the verse commentaries by all three women, were then compiled into a collection, and the literatus-official and Buddhist layman Zhang Dayuan 張大圓 (1589–1669), who knew and admired Baochi and Zukui, wrote a preface for it and arranged

---

1. Chan Buddhist masters normally have several names. Miaozong, for example, is also referred to as Wuzhuo Miaozong 無著妙總 or Zeshou Miaozong 資壽妙總; Baochi as Baochi Jizong 寶持濟總 or Baochi Xuanzong 寶持玄總; and Zukui as Zukui Jifu 祖揆濟符. In order to avoid confusion, I have chosen to refer to them in this book simply as Miaozong, Baochi, and Zukui.

for it to be printed.² It is unclear how widely the printed collection circulated as an independent text, but fortunately it was considered important enough to be included in the *Jiaxing Canon* (*Jiaxing dazangjing* 嘉興大藏經), a multi-volume collection of Buddhist canonical writings collated and printed during the end of the seventeenth century and the beginning of the eighteenth.³ There they have lain tucked away since then, largely unnoticed and, until now, never translated into English.

Of primary interest in this book are the verses: the kōans to which they are written are all relatively well known, and annotated English translations of most of them are widely available.⁴ For this reason, and because this book is intended primarily for a general audience, I have not provided overly detailed annotations of either the kōans or the verses. It is also important to note that while these verse commentaries are unique in being authored by female Chan masters, this is not to say that they offer a distinctively female perspective on the Chan experience. But perhaps they should not be expected to, since this experience was, theoretically at least, supposed to be one unmarked by gender distinctions. What they do offer is an eloquent illustration of the fact that, in a religious milieu made up overwhelmingly of men, there were women who were just as dedicated to Chan practice, just as advanced in their spiritual realization, and just as gifted at using language to convey that which is beyond language.

---

2. Zhang Dayuan is the religious name of Zhang Youyu 張有譽, an official who passed the highest imperial examinations in 1622 and who subsequently held a number of fairly prominent posts. (Zhang is his surname, which, as is customary in Chinese, comes before the given name.) After the fall of the Ming dynasty to the Manchus in 1644, Zhang, like so many other loyalist scholar-officials of the time, quit office and turned to Buddhism. He dedicated himself completely to his religious practice and study, lecturing and writing commentaries on Buddhist scriptures. Zhang's preface is especially valuable because he clearly knew the two women personally, and although he was primarily interested in praising the work, he does provide a few biographical details about their lives not found elsewhere.

3. In China, there were many different collections and editions of Buddhist canonical works, which included both works translated from Indian and Central Asian sources and works composed in China itself. Baochi and Zukui's collection of verses is found only in one of these, the *Jiaxing Canon*. See CBETA J28, B215: 565a3–571b26.

4. For an excellent selection of studies on the kōan, see Steven Heine and Dale S. Wright, *The Kōan: Texts and Contexts in Zen Buddhism* (Oxford and New York: Oxford University Press, 2000).

The popular, if undoubtedly romanticized, image of the Chan master responding to a bewildered student's earnest queries with seemingly irrelevant statements, or alternatively, with deafening shouts and painful blows, was largely a literary product of Song dynasty China (960–1279). It was in the Song that the biographies, sermons, and above all, records of the lively encounters with great masters of the Tang dynasty (618–907) such as Linji 臨濟 and Mazu 馬祖 were widely collected, compiled (and sometimes elaborated or even invented) and circulated as individual texts.[5] In addition, selections of these texts were collected in comprehensive anthologies, one of the first of which was *The Jingde Transmission of the Lamp* (*Jingde chuandeng lu* 景德傳燈錄) published in 1004. This collection was followed by numerous other "lamp transmissions," as well as anthologies comprised of accounts selected from these larger collections and designed primarily for the purpose of training Chan practitioners, although they were also widely appreciated by educated lay readers who may or may not have been interested in engaging in intensive Chan practice. These selected accounts, often in the form of so-called encounter dialogues between master and disciple, came to be known as *kōan* (the Japanese pronunciation of the Chinese term *gong'an* 公案, which means, literally, "public case" or "precedent"). By the Song dynasty, it became common practice for commentaries in both prose and verse to be appended to these kōans. These commentaries were for the most part written by men who were Chan masters themselves, and as such could inspire and instruct aspiring students of the Way as much as the original cases themselves.

One of the earliest of these anthologies was *Xuedou's Collection of Verse Commentaries* (*Xuedou songgu ji* 雪竇頌古集) compiled by the Song dynasty Chan master Xuedou Zhongxian 雪竇重顯 (980–1052). It was comprised of one hundred cases, the great majority of which were selected from the *The Jingde Transmission of the Lamp* collection mentioned above. Xuedou, who had received a classical Confucian literary education before becoming ordained at the age of twenty-three, often chose to write his

5. For two excellent English translations of one of the most famous individual collections of this kind, see *The Record of Linji*, translated and commentary by Ruth Fuller Sasaki, edited by Thomas Yūhō Kirchner (Honolulu: University of Hawai'i Press, 2009) and Burton Watson, trans. *The Zen Teachings of Master Lin-Chi* (New York: Columbia University Press, 1999).

commentaries in verse. Although he was not the first to do so, it is with Xuedou that the verse commentary emerged as a fully distinct genre of Chinese Chan literature.[6]

Several decades after its publication, we find Xuedou's collection of cases being used extensively by Chan Master Yuanwu Keqin 圜悟克勤 (1063–1135) as a basis for his own teachings. Yuanwu Keqin added his own commentaries to those made by Xuedou, and together they would become the anthology that in English is often translated as *The Blue Cliff Record* (*Biyan lu* 碧岩錄).[7] *The Blue Cliff Record* inspired several other similar anthologies of cases appended by commentaries in both verse and prose, such as *The Gateless Gate* (*Wumen guan* 無門關), a collection of forty-eight cases compiled by Chan Master Wumen Huikai 無門慧開 (1183–1260), and published in 1228, and *The Book of Serenity* (*Congrong lu* 從容錄) compiled by Chan Master Wansong Xingxiu 萬松行秀 (1166–1246).

These three anthologies, and especially the first two, enjoyed a great popularity in East Asia, not only among monastic Chan practitioners, but also the educated elite who delighted in the poetic, if often puzzling, language of these texts. In fact, so great was their popularity that some Chan teachers, including Chan Master Dahui Zonggao 大慧宗杲 (1089–1163), generally regarded to be the greatest of all the Song dynasty masters and a Dharma heir of Yuanwu Keqin himself, began to worry that their literary attractions were more of a hindrance than an aid to realization—it's said that he even went so far as to destroy his copy of *The Blue Cliff Record* and strongly caution his disciples against reading it. Dahui is known for his use of a practice that involved not meditating on (much less memorizing) a complete kōan, but rather using a single word or phrase (referred to in Chinese as *huatou* 話頭) from the kōan as a tool with which to overcome the limitations of purely discursive thought and experience a reality unbounded by words. For instance, one of the most famous kōan is an encounter dialogue that already seems to be pared down to its absolute

6. For a useful discussion of these types of poetic genres, see Ding-hwa Hsieh, "Poetry and Chan 'Gong'an': From Xuedou Chongxian (980–1052) to Wumen Huikai (1183–1260)," *Journal of Song-Yuan Studies* 40 (2010): 39–70.

7. For a popular and easily accessible English translation of this important collection, see Thomas Cleary and J.C. Cleary, trans., *The Blue Cliff Record* (Boston and London: Shambhala Publications, 1992).

essentials: A monk asked Zhaozhou, "Does a dog have Buddha-nature or not?" Zhaozhou replied, "He does not." Dahui, however, pares it down even further, and selects the key phrase "He does not," which in Chinese is just one word: *wu* 無 (in Japanese pronounced "*mu*"). It is with this word that the practitioner must grapple, with a great intensity and sense of urgency, building up a tremendous "great doubt" that, if all goes well, will at some point result in a shattering insight into the true nature of reality. This method of meditative inquiry on the huatou did not originate with Dahui. However, it was he who is largely responsible for perfecting and popularizing its use—in many cases with the help of some of his female disciples, among whom the most well known was none other than Miaozong, the first of the three women Chan masters whose verse commentaries are translated in this book.[8]

After Dahui, the use of the huatou became central to many forms of Chan practice, especially in the Linji (Rinzai in Japanese) school. Nevertheless, anthologies comprised of kōans accompanied by verse and prose commentaries such as *The Blue Cliff Record* continued to be read, studied, and savored by lay and monastic alike. Moreover, many of the individual collections of writings and sermons (known as "discourse records" or *yulu*, 語錄) of Chan masters from the twelfth century down to recent times include entire sections of verse commentaries. Such was the popularity of these verses even in the Song dynasty that a Chan monk by the name of Faying 法應 (exact dates unknown) devoted thirty years of his life to collecting 2,100 verses by 122 different Chan monks. This collection, the original edition of which is unfortunately no longer extant, was published in 1175 under the title of *The String of Pearls Collection of Verses from the Chan School* (*Chanzong songgu lianzhu ji* 禪宗頌古聯珠集). Nearly a century later, an otherwise unknown Yuan dynasty (1271–1368) monk

8. For more on Dahui's teaching methods, see Miriam Levering, "Dahui Zonggao (1089–1163): The Image Created by His Stories about Himself and by His Teaching Style," in *Zen Masters*, eds. Steven Heine and Dale Wright (Oxford and New York: Oxford University Press, 2010), 91–116. There is also much good scholarship on the use of the huatou in Chan meditation practice. A good place to begin is Robert Buswell's article "The 'Short-Cut' Approach of K'an-hua Meditation: The Evolution of a Practical Subitism in Chinese Ch'an Buddhism," in *Sudden and Gradual: Approaches to Enlightenment in Chinese Thought*, ed., Peter N. Gregory (Honolulu: University of Hawai'i Press, 1987), 321–77.

by the name of Puhui 普會 edited and expanded Faying's original collection, resulting in an anthology composed of 3,050 verses by 426 different authors. Published in 1317 under the title of *The Comprehensive String of Pearls Collection of Verse Commentaries from the Chan School* (*Chanzong songgu lianzhu tongji* 禪宗頌古聯珠通集), this expanded collection was eventually incorporated into the Chinese Buddhist Canon, where it can be found today. Among the verses added by Puhui were many composed after the 1175 publication of Faying's original collection—including, for the first time, the verses composed by Miaozong, the most well known of the three female Dharma successors of Dahui Zonggao. It is these verses that, many centuries later, would inspire the seventeenth-century nuns Baochi and Zukui to each compose verses in response both to the original cases selected by Miaozong and to the verses she wrote to accompany them.

CHAN MASTER MIAOZONG

Miaozong was arguably the most well known of the three women Dharma heirs of the eminent Song dynasty Chan master Dahui Zonggao (to whom I will refer simply as Dahui from now on). Dahui was a teacher who both nourished and acknowledged the spiritual potential of his female disciples. In the numerous collections of his sermons, letters, and writings, one can find numerous accounts of his interactions with his women students, including at least fourteen nuns and twenty-seven laywomen. In one Dharma instruction, for example, we find him telling a female lay disciple about Miaozong's spiritual attainments and suggesting that if the disciple made a real effort, she might well become a second Miaozong.[9] (Nearly five centuries later, we find Zhang Dayuan claiming that Baochi and Zukui had indeed achieved this goal and could be regarded as spiritual "reincarnations" of their twelfth-century predecessor.)

The most important source for biographical information regarding Miaozong is a biographical account found in the *Precious Mirror of Gods and Humans* (*Rentian baojian* 人天寶鑑) compiled by the Northern Song

---

9. "To the Wife of the District Magistrate of Yongning" ("Shi Yongning Jun furen 示永寧郡夫人") in *Chan Master Dahui Pujue's Dharma Talks* (*Dahui Pujue chanshi fayu* 大慧普覺禪師法語), CBETA T47, 1998A: 903c8–904c13.

dynasty poet-monk Tanxiu 曇秀 and first published in 1230.[10] The information provided by Tanxiu's account, when supplemented by additional bits of information gleaned from other sources, and in particular, the writings and letters of Dahui himself, makes it possible to paint a fairly detailed portrait of Miaozong.[11]

Miaozong came from a very illustrious and scholarly family: her grandfather, for example, was the scholar-official Su Song 蘇頌 (1020–1101), who after passing the highest national civil examinations in 1042, subsequently held a series of high official posts, including that of Vice Prime Minister. Su Song was a veritable polymath, known among other things for his poetry writing, his art collecting, and his scholarship in the areas of astronomy, pharmacology, and cartography. He was also a mechanical genius of sorts, famous for having devised, and later written a treatise about, a water-driven astronomical clock. While we know very little about Miaozong's early life, we can assume that, like other women of her time who were born to distinguished gentry families and unlike most of their less-privileged sisters, she was afforded a solid education, which included studying the classic works of Chinese literature, philosophy, and history, and learning to write poetry. In this account, we are told that even as an adolescent, Miaozong had already begun to ponder such existential questions such as where and what we are before we take birth, and where and what we will be after we die. After contemplating these questions with great intensity, she apparently had what one might call a first experience of awakened insight. Unaware that this experience represented anything out of the ordinary, she kept it to herself and dutifully acquiesced to her family's arrangements for her to be married to a young scholar-official from a good family like hers. Even after marriage, Miaozong's early religious

---

10. This collection can be found at CBETA X87, 1612: 21b2–c18.
11. This is precisely what Miriam Levering has done in the composite biography of Miaozong that she provides in her article "Women Ch'an Masters: The Teacher Miao-tsung as Saint," in *Women Saints in World Religions*, ed. Arvind Sharma (Albany, NY: State University of New York Press, 2000) 180–204, as well as in "The Biography of Miaozong (translation)," in *Zen Sourcebook: Traditional Documents from China, Korea, and Japan*, eds. Stephen Addiss, Stanley Lombardo, and Judith Roitman (Indianapolis/Cambridge: Hackett Publishing Company, 2008), 126–31. The portrait of Miaozong I offer here draws heavily on Levering's invaluable and path-breaking research, for which I am immensely grateful.

inclinations continued unabated, and she began to visit different eminent Chan monks in search of spiritual guidance.

According to Tanxiu, one of these masters opened their interview by asking Miaozong pointblank, "How can a beautiful woman from the inner quarters expect to engage in the matters of great gentleman?" Miaozong's reply was equally straightforward: "Is the Buddhadharma divided into male and female forms?" Master and student then embarked on a "Dharma exchange" from which, we are told, Miaozong emerged victorious. In the Dharma instruction addressed to one of his female lay disciples quoted earlier, Dahui even goes so far as to state that Miaozong received confirmation of her enlightenment from each and every one of the eminent masters that she visited during this time.

Although after her marriage Miaozong visited many eminent masters from the Jiangsu and Zhejiang area, she did not meet Dahui until sometime in 1137 when she was living in Jiahe 嘉禾 (present-day Jiaxing 嘉興, in Zhejiang province), where her husband had been assigned a new official post. It so happened that around this time, Dahui happened to stop in Jiahe on his way to take up a post as abbot at a monastery on Mount Jing 徑山, located just outside of Hangzhou. When Miaozong heard about this, she immediately went to pay her respects, but when she saw Dahui, she simply bowed and left without saying a word. Something about her caught Dahui's attention, however, and turning to a lay official who had studied with Dahui for many years and who was now accompanying him on his journey, he remarked, "That laywoman who was just here has definitely seen something that is as startling as a ghost or spirit. However, because she has yet to face the hammer and tongs, the forge and bellows, like a ten-thousand-ton ship in a blocked harbor, she is still unable budge." In other words, Dahui recognized that Miaozong had already attained a degree of realization, but that without the guidance and challenge of a master, she would be able to go no further.

It was customary for local officials to request visiting monks, especially if they were as eminent as Dahui, to deliver a public sermon while they were in the area. Thus it happened that the following day, Miaozong's husband—perhaps at the urging of his wife—invited Dahui to give a Dharma talk. Both he and his wife were in attendance, of course, and at one point in his talk—again according to Tanxiu's account—Dahui looked out over the assembled audience and said, "Today among you there is a person who has seen something. I inspect people as would a customs official— no sooner do I see them coming, then I know whether or not they have dutiable goods." After the talk was over, Miaozong, knowing that she was the person being referred to, approached Dahui and requested that he select a Dharma name for her, thus indicating her desire to study with him. Dahui then gave her the Dharma name Wuzhuo 無著, which means "nonattachment."

The connection made, the following year, Miaozong made her way to Mount Jing, where Dahui was now living, in order to participate in the three-month intensive summer retreat.[12] Miaozong's subsequent exchanges, or so-called "Dharma battles," with Dahui in many ways form the heart of her biographical accounts, as indeed they do of most biographies/hagiographies of eminent monastics, and would become quite famous. Dahui himself describes many of these exchanges in his own writings, often using them to instruct and inspire other practitioners, especially other female practitioners. One of the first of these, which I here paraphrase rather than translate, took place during the summer retreat mentioned above.

According to Dahui's account, during one of his sermons he raised the story of Yaoshan Weiyan 藥山惟儼 (774–827) who, intrigued by this new Chan teaching that claimed not to rely on study of the scriptures, went to the great master Shitou Xiqian 石頭希遷 (700–790) seeking further elucidation.[13] However, instead of explaining it to Yaoshan, Shitou simply commented: "Being this way won't do; not being this way won't do. Being this way and not being this way both won't do." Seeing Yaoshan's utter confusion, Shitou sent him off to the great Mazu and eventually Yaoshan "got it." As she listened to Dahui recount this story of Yaoshan and Shitou, Miaozong also "got it," although she at first she kept her realization to

---

12. Dahui notes that there were 1,700 monastics participating in the summer retreat on Mt. Jing that summer. Given that most of these monastics were probably male, and that Miaozong was still a laywoman at this point, this makes her accomplishments that much more remarkable.

13. This information also appears in Dahui's letter, "To the Wife of the District Magistrate of Yongning."

herself. However, another member of the congregation, an official and lay practitioner, was convinced that he too had "got it," went immediately to Dahui's quarters and said, "I understand it!" When Dahui asked him how it was he understood it, the official replied by restating Shitou's enigmatic words, although with the addition of three strings of Sanskrit syllables transliterated into Chinese, none of which have any clear meaning: "Being this way won't do, *soro shabaho*. Being that way won't do, *xili shabaho*. Being this way won't do and not being this way both won't do, *soro xili shabaho*." When Dahui heard this, he refrained from either confirming or rejecting the official's insight. Later, however, he asked Miaozong what she thought of the man's words. She laughed and, as if to change the subject, said, "Guo Xiang commented on Zhuangzi 莊子. Those who know say that it was actually Zhuangzi who commented on Guo Xiang." Guo Xiang 郭象 (d. 312) was the author of an unfinished commentary to the famous classical Daoist text known as the *Zhuangzi* attributed to the fourth-century BCE philosopher Zhuang Zhou 莊周, who was also known as Zhuangzi or Master Zhuang. By reversing the roles of author and commentator, Miaozong may have been suggesting that the official's "comment" on Shitou's original statement was inadequate, to say the least. And, of course, by so suggesting, she was demonstrating to Dahui that her own insight was more on target. Although Dahui clearly agreed, instead of saying as much he too shifted the topic of conversation, this time asking her about a story involving Chan Master Yantou Quanhuo 嚴頭全奯 (828–87).

This story, another version of which appears later as case 33, tells how Yantou worked for a while as a ferryman transporting people back and forth across a lake.[14] One day a woman passenger carrying a baby in her arms turned to Yantou and asked, "Where did this baby that I am holding in my arms come from?" Yantou replied, in good Chan master fashion, by smacking her with his oar. Unfazed, the woman said, "I have already given birth to seven children, six of whom never encountered a true friend. Nor will it be any different with this one." And so saying, she threw the child into the water.

---

14. For another translation of this story, see Thomas Yūhō Kirchner, *Entangling Vines: A Classic Collection of Zen Kōans* (Boston: Wisdom Publications, 2013), 140.

The deeper meaning of this rather horrifying tale most likely hinges on the word "true friend" (*zhiyin* 知音), which literally means "someone who understands the sound." The expression refers to a famous story of a man who could always and immediately understand the feeling behind his friend's zither-playing—so much so that when he died, his musician friend, despairing of ever again being understood in this way, broke the strings of his instrument and never played again. In Miaozong's verse, the true friend refers to someone on the same spiritual wavelength: in other words, the mind-to-mind connection that Miaozong appears to have established not only with the ancient Tang master Shitou, but also with Dahui himself.

Writing a verse to give to the master was a traditional way for a student to articulate his or her understanding, and Miaozong responded to the story of Yantou with what would later come to be regarded as one of her signature verses:

A leaf of a boat drifts across the vast stretch of water;
Lifting and dancing his oars, he sings to a different tune.
Mountain clouds and ocean moon: both are tossed away;
The battle won, Zhuang Zhou's butterfly dream carries on.

In this verse, Miaozong plays on the images of boat and oar from the story of Yantou the ferryman, although what is tossed into the waters is, somewhat more poetically, not a baby but rather the clouds over the mountain and the moon over the sea. She also indirectly echoes her earlier comment regarding Guo Xiang and the *Zhuangzi* by referring to the famous story about how Zhuang Zhou the philosopher, upon waking from a dream in which he was a butterfly, wonders if perhaps he is now a butterfly dreaming he is a human. Miaozong also echoes the sound metaphor implicit in the term "true friend" with the phrase "he sings a different tune"—which is often used in Chan to refer to someone who has come to experience the world with an awakened mind. In this way, all the elements of the "Dharma battle" between Dahui and Miaozong—stories, questions, comments, and poem—become an affirmation of her spiritual insight.

On yet another teaching occasion, Miaozong offered Dahui the follow-ing verse:

> In a flash, I have touched the very tip of my nose;
> All my clever tricks have melted like ice and shattered like tiles.
> What need was there for Bodhidharma to come from the West?
> The Second Patriarch bowed to him three times all for nothing!
> If you still insist on asking what is this and how it could be:
> An entire brigade of straw bandits has suffered a huge defeat!

In the poem he wrote in response to this one, Dahui explicitly acknowl-edges Miaozong's awakening, something he had not done before. Dahui's poem reads as follows:

> Since you have awakened to the living intention of the patriarchs,
> Cut everything in two with a single stroke, and finish off the job.
> Facing karmic occasions one by one, trust to your original nature;
> Whether in the world or out of it, there is neither excess nor lack.
> I compose this verse as a confirmation of your awakening.
> The four types of awakened beings and the six unawakened
>   may worry,[15]
> But you needn't worry—even the blue-eyed barbarian has yet
>   to get it![16]

Up until now, we have talked solely about Miaozong's encounters with her teacher, Dahui. However, there is a story (and it may indeed be only a story) of a very different sort of an encounter, found in a preface to a poem in a 1254 anthology of Chan writings. It tells of an encounter between Miaozong and Wan'an Daoyan 卍菴道顔 (1094–1164), the head monk at Mount Jing who would also become one of Dahui's Dharma

---

15. The four types of awakened beings refer to the śrāvaka, the pratyekabuddha, the bodhisattva, and the Buddha; the six types of unawakened beings refer to the denizens of the six realms of samsara: hell-beings, hungry ghosts, animals, asuras, humans, and gods.
16. The blue-eyed barbarian refers to the semi-legendary figure of Bodhidharma, tradition-ally regarded as the First Patriarch of Chan.

heirs.[17] Wan'an is described as disapproving of this woman and of the fact that his teacher had gone so far as to allow her to stay in the abbot's quarters. Aware of his male disciple's feelings, Dahui insists that Wan'an call on Miaozong himself. When the monk shows up at her door, Miaozong asked him whether theirs is to be a worldly meeting or a Dharma meeting. When Wan'an assures her that it will be the latter, Miaozong tells him to dismiss his attendants and then goes back into her room. A little later, she calls for him to enter, and when he does, he finds her lying stretched out on her bed completely naked. The shocked monk then points at her exposed private parts and asks, "What kind of place is this?" "The buddhas of the three worlds, the six patriarchs, and the great monks everywhere all emerge from here," answers Miaozong. Wan'an then asks whether or not he will be allowed to enter, to which Miaozong cuttingly replies, "It allows horses to cross, but it does not allow asses to do so." When Wan'an does not respond, Miaozong declares the interview over and turns over on her side. The embarrassed monk, not knowing what else to do, quickly leaves the room. When Wan'an later tells Dahui about this shocking meeting with Miaozong, Dahui remarks, "It is certainly not the case that that old beast lacks insight!" And so again we see Miaozong presumably operating on a level of understanding that far surpassed many of Dahui's male disciples, whether monastic or lay.

When Dahui recounts his exchanges with Miaozong during her first summer retreat with him, he refers to her as Madame Xu, which means that she was still a laywoman at that time. In fact, it was not until 1163, the year Dahui died and most likely after her husband had died as well, that Miaozong was officially ordained as a nun. At this point she was quite advanced in years and no doubt planned to spend the rest of her life in seclusion. However, she had already become quite famous and greatly admired for her spiritual insight and strict discipline. As a result she was asked to serve as abbess of the Zeshou Nunnery 資壽庵, which was located on the outskirts of what is today the city of Shanghai.

A number of sermons delivered by Miaozong during her time as abbess

---

17. This anecdote appears in a 1254 collection entitled *Poems of Appraisal of the Correct Tradition of the Five Schools* (*Wujia zhengzong zan* 五家正宗贊) by the Song dynasty Chan monk Shaotan 紹曇 (d. 1298). CBETA X78, 1554: 598b20–c7.

have been preserved, as well as a handful of Dharma exchanges with her students.[18] The first sermon she gave upon ascending to her new position, a portion of which I have translated below, provides a sense of the religious authority—the authority of a Chan master—with which she taught:

> Once the essential teaching of Chan is conveyed, then that of the Buddhist Canon is completely finished. Once the command of the patriarchs is carried out, then the ten directions are completely cut off. When the two vehicles hear it, they flee in fear. When the bodhisattvas of the ten stages reach it, they still doubt. The best of the lot, however, will understand without being told. Even methods powerful enough to shift the placement of the stars and constellations, and stratagems that can appropriate the enemy's flag and drums—even these are no more than the show of empty fists. How could they be of any real significance? When it comes to the path to transcendence, sages do not transmit anything, and students do nothing but toil over forms, like monkeys grasping at their own reflections. What Śākyamuni Buddha transmitted at Vulture Peak came at an opportune time. He elaborated upon the three vehicles, each according to the faculties and capacities of his listeners. Beginning at the Deer Park with his teaching of the four noble truths, he ferried hundreds of thousands of beings [across the river of samsara]. Today I, the mountain monastic—together with this world and all other worlds, with the buddhas and patriarchs, with the mountains, rivers and great Earth, the grasses and trees, woods and forests—appear before the four-fold assembly, each of us turning the great wheel of Dharma. Everyone's radiances blend and crisscross like a jeweled silken net. If there be a single blade of grass, a single tree, that does not turn the

---

18. Many of Miaozong's sermons, including this one, can be found in the brief biographical notice included in the *Jiatai Record of the Universal Lamps* (*Jiatai pudenglu* 嘉泰普燈錄), which was published in 1204 (the fourth year of the Jiatai period of the Song dynasty). CBETA X79, 1559: 405a11–c8.

wheel of Dharma, then one cannot call my sermon today a true turning of the great wheel of Dharma. . . ."

Miaozong only resided at the Zeshou Nunnery for a few years before she retired, and in 1170 she died at the age of 76. Although long lost, there does appear to have been a collection of her sermons, poems, and other writings published before her death,[19] and it is possible that the verse commentaries later collected in Puhui's Yuan dynasty anthology may have been culled from this earlier collection. Most importantly, Miaozong's fame as a realized female Chan master would continue to inspire later generations of spiritual aspirants—in particular women who might otherwise feel that the demanding, and in many ways highly masculine, practices of Chan were beyond their capabilities.

CHAN MASTER BAOCHI AND CHAN MASTER ZUKUI

Baochi and Zukui were two of a small number of seventeenth-century women who, although by no means as famous as Miaozong, were also recognized Dharma successors of eminent male masters, in this case the Linji Chan master Jiqi Hongchu 繼起弘儲 (1605–72).[20] Jiqi Hongchu was a second-generation Dharma successor of Chan Master Miyun Yuanwu 密雲圓悟 (1566–1642), generally regarded as the primary force behind a lively if short-lived revival of the Linji school of Chan Buddhism.[21] He received a solid classical Confucian education but left home and became a monk when he was in his mid-twenties. After receiving Dharma transmission, he served as abbot of several major Buddhist monasteries before retiring to spend the latter years of his life on Mount Lingyan 靈嚴 just outside the

---

19. Such records existed for other Song dynasty nuns, some of whom were known and admired for their erudition and eloquence, as well. For more, see Evelyn Ding-hwa Hsieh, "Buddhist Nuns in Sung China." *Journal of Sung-Yuan Studies* 30 (2000): 63–96.
20. For more a much more detailed discussion on these and other nuns from this period, see Grant, *Eminent Nuns: Women Chan Masters of Seventeenth-Century China* (Honolulu: University of Hawai'i Press, 2009).
21. For a path-breaking study of this revival, see Jiang Wu, *Enlightenment in Dispute: The Reinvention of Chan Buddhism in Seventeenth-Century China* (New York and Oxford: Oxford University Press, 2011).

famous city of Suzhou in southeastern China. Known both for his literary talents and his fervent loyalist sympathies, Jiqi Hongchu had many disciples, including many lay followers like the official-literatus Zhang Dayuan, the author of the preface to this translated collection of verses. Baochi and Zukui, however, appear to be the only two women to whom he granted Dharma transmission.

As Chan masters, Baochi and Zukui were both entitled, and indeed expected, to have their own discourse records, which include some of their sermons, poems, and other writings. These records have, fortunately, been preserved in the Jiaxing Buddhist Canon. As interesting and valuable as these records are, they do not, however, provide very much biographical information about these two nuns. Other types of sources, in particular local gazetteers, yield a bit more information, although mostly about Baochi who had earned a reputation as a loyal wife and wise mother, not to mention a talented poet and painter, before she entered the religious life in late middle age. About Zukui's life, unfortunately, we know very little, although her religious writings are the richer and more numerous of the two.

Baochi was born in Jiaxing, and until she became a nun was known as Jin Shuxiu 金淑秀, although in order to avoid confusion, she will be referred to here by her religious name of Baochi. In fact, in biographical notices found in official gazetteers, mention is sometimes made of her piety, but almost never of the fact that she actually became a Buddhist nun and Chan master. Like Miaozong, she came from an elite family known for its scholarship. Her father was a fairly high-ranking official known for his literary talents, but he was known especially for his personal integrity and loyalty to the Ming court, which by the first half of the seventeenth century was on its last legs and would be officially replaced in 1644 by the Manchu Qing dynasty.

Baochi early on acquired a reputation for being an exemplary filial daughter, caring for her widowed mother and, after the untimely death of her brother, along with his young wife and two daughters. She is also described as having been an intellectually precocious young girl who later became known in particular for her artistic talents. In fact, her talent would earn her an entry in a major collection of biographies of eminent artists compiled by Zhang Geng 張庚 (1685–1760) and published in 1739. According to Zhang, who only commented on works that he had actually seen personally, Baochi was especially good at painting landscapes, which he characterizes as being imbued with a "manly spirit" (*zhangfu qi* 丈夫氣).[22]

Baochi's family arranged a marriage for her with Xu Zhaosen 許肇森, who came from a family even more famous than her own for its scholarship, official service, and loyalism. In 1640, Zhaosen's father perished along with more than twenty members of his immediate family in a valiant attempt to defend his city from the havoc and destruction being wreaked by the infamous rebel Zhang Xianzhong 張獻忠 (1605–47). After the massacre of his family, Zhaosen received an honorary post of Minister in the Directorate of Education; his primary interest, however, lay in ensuring that his father's heroism not be forgotten, and Baochi greatly assisted him in this work, even going so far as to sell her jewelry in order to help support them financially. However, Zhaosen does not appear to have outlived his father by very long, and Baochi was left a widow with at least four children. One of her sons, Xu Jiayan 徐嘉炎 (1631–1703), would go on to a brilliant career as a scholar, official, and poet. After his father's death, Jiayan built a small chapel for his mother on the grounds of his home in the eastern suburbs of Jiaxing; this chapel would later become the Miaozhan Chan Nunnery 妙湛禪院. It is unclear when exactly Baochi actually decided to seek ordination as a Buddhist nun. However, she may well have been encouraged to do so by the woman who during this time, and perhaps even earlier, was her friend and confidante: the woman we know primarily as Chan Master Zukui.

Unfortunately, we have very little biographical information about Zukui despite the fact that, in addition to her verses in *The Concordant Sounds Collection*, she has left us two five-chapter collections of writings (as opposed to Baochi's relatively slim two-chapter collection). This paucity of information may be due to the fact that Zukui became a Buddhist nun without ever having married or simply that her family connections were

---

22. Cited in Yu Jianhua, *People's Dictionary of Chinese Artists* (*Zhongguo meishujia renming cidian*) (Shanghai: Renming meishu chubanshe, 1981), 557.

not enough to merit her much mention in official gazetteers. All we know for certain is that she was born in the city Huzhou 湖州, which was named for its proximity to the scenic Lake Tai (or Taihu 太湖), in northern Zhejiang province; that her family name was Li 李; and that, like Baochi, she was known for her intellectual precocity and literary talents even as a young girl.

Baochi always refers to Zukui as "elder brother" (in China, it was customary for female monastics to refer to each other using male kinship terms), suggesting either that Zukui was older than Baochi or perhaps simply that she had entered the religious life before Baochi. It is also unclear how or when the two women came to know each other, although it is possible that they were related either by blood or by marriage. At some point, Zukui became the abbess of the Lingrui Nunnery 靈瑞菴, which, from references in her poems and other writings, would appear to have been located in the hills bordering Lake Tai—in other words, not too far from her birthplace.

Zhang Dayuan describes in his preface how the two women could often be found reading and discussing Chan Buddhist texts together. One of the texts they found particularly inspiring was a recently printed compilation by Chan Master Jiqi Hongchu, who by this time had retired to Mount Lingyan, located near Suzhou.[23] Zhang writes:

> Every day from dawn to dusk [Baochi] studied with the abbess Zukui. She practiced hard and with great determination. One day she happened to be reading Jiqi Hongchu of Lingyan's discourse records, and it was as if the warmth of the springtime sun had suddenly penetrated into a wintry valley. She immediately went to ask for an audience with the elderly monk who, as soon as he saw her, saw she had the qualities of a "manly man." (da zhangfu 大丈夫).

23. It is not clear which collection Baochi and Zukui read as there are several such collections associated with Jiqi Hongchu that would have been in circulation during this time. It is quite likely, however, that they were reading the master's own discourse record collection for which he himself wrote a short preface dated 1671, the year before his death, but which was probably in circulation well before that time.

Zhang claims that Jiqi immediately recognized Baochi's religious potential, referring to her as a "manly man": someone with the strength and determination to engage in serious Chan practice. This highly gendered rhetoric can be found in many Chan Buddhist texts and was used to refer not only to men but also to exceptional women regarded as honorary men—as we have seen, Baochi's painting was also described has having a "manly spirit."

It would appear from Zhang's preface that Baochi began to devote herself to the study of Chan texts even before the death of her husband, and that her first visit to Master Jiqi was as a laywoman. As we read further in the preface, we find that it was not until after her husband died and was buried that she returned to Mount Lingyan where she would take ordination. According to Zhang, Baochi proved to be an exceptionally dedicated student. He writes that every time Jiqi gave her an instruction—probably a huatou or critical phrase for her to contemplate—Baochi would forgo both sleeping and eating in order to grapple with it.

It was after one of these periods of intensive practice that Baochi had her "enlightenment experience," which was confirmed by the elderly Jiqi Hongchu, who shortly afterward also named her an official Dharma successor. Baochi then appears to have returned home to her family chapel, now the Miaozhan Chan Nunnery, where she resided as abbess until she was invited to head the nearby Nanxun Chan Nunnery 南詢禪院. (Zukui took her place as abbess of Miaozhan when Baochi left.) However, Baochi would always be associated primarily with the Miaozhan Nunnery; she is often referred to as Miaozhan Baochi.

We have a record of Zukui presiding over a memorial service for Baochi, so we know that the latter died first. After Baochi passed away, her disciples compiled a collection of some of her sermons, poems, and other writings. The preface for this collection was written by the monk Sengjian Xiaoqing 僧鑒曉青 (1629–90), the Dharma successor of Jiqi Hongchu who had assumed leadership of the monastery on Mount Lingyan after his teacher's death in 1672. In his rather fulsome preface, Sengjian praises both Baochi's spiritual and her literary achievements, which he sees as being two sides of a single coin. He writes:

The peerless and marvelous Way does not depend on language and yet it does not separate itself from language: To seek for it by clinging to language is like grasping a flower and thinking that one thus captured the springtime. However, if one seeks for it by doing away completely with words, it will be like seeking the springtime by throwing away the flowers! To speak of either clinging or renouncing is a product of confused thinking and does not represent the true and correct view. Reading these discourse records is also like this: if you say that the way of Master [Baochi] is completely contained in them, you do not know the master. But if you say that the way of the master is not to be found in them, you also do not know the Master. . . . You should penetrate into each word and each phrase, and touch that which is beyond all words and phrases. Only then will you be faithful to the original intention of these words left by the Master.

Unlike Baochi, Zukui saw her two five-chapter collections printed and in circulation before her death. The first of these is titled *The Miaozhan Records of the Nun of Lingrui, Chan Master Zukui Fu* (*Lingrui ni Zukui Fu Chanshi Miaozhan lu* 靈瑞尼祖揆符禪師妙湛錄). As the title indicates, this collection was compiled sometime during Zukui's tenure as abbess of the Miaozhan Chan Nunnery. The second collection is titled *Chan Master of Lingrui's Cliffside Flowers Collection* (*Lingrui chanshi Yanhua ji* 靈瑞禪師嚴華集) and is comprised of materials that were probably composed while she was in residence at the Lingrui Nunnery, where she had resided before taking up the leadership of the Miaozhan Chan Nunnery, and where she may well have returned to spend her last days. Zhang Dayuan also wrote a preface for Zukui's *Cliffside Flowers Collection*. In this preface, dated 1661, Zhang praises Zukui with the same exuberance he claims for the nun's own writing:

The words that come from the mouth of the great master from Lingrui are dashing and bold, her tongue is overflowing and exuberant. Sometimes she takes the entire ocean and squeezes it into a single drop, thus completely drying up the universe. . . .

at other times she takes a single drop and expands it into an entire ocean extending over the past and the present without impediment and without deliberation.

Even a cursory perusal of these two collections points to Zukui's deep familiarity—one might even say intimacy—with the words and deeds of the great Tang masters as described in texts from the Song dynasty onward. Just to give an example, she writes a long series of quatrains entitled "On a Spring Day, Thinking of the Masters of the Past," each one of which plays poetically on an episode or teaching from a different Tang dynasty master. Zukui was also extremely fond of the *The Blue Cliff Record*, the famous Song dynasty anthology, and even wrote a series of verse commentaries on each of its one hundred cases.

Apart from being fellow disciples of Master Jiqi Hongchu, Baochi and Zukui also shared a strong literary friendship. In their respective collections, for example, one finds a great many poems using the rhymes, title, and topics of each other's verses, as well as poems written to and about each other. Given their literary interests and their shared passion for reading and discussing such anthologies as *The Blue Cliff Record*, it is not surprising that they might be inspired to produce a similar anthology. It is not clear where they had come across the verses of their famous predecessor Miaozong; that is, whether there may have been a now-lost self-contained collection of Miaozong's verses in circulation or whether they culled them from the extant anthologies of such verses. In any case, they decided that they would each write a verse to the same forty-three Chan cases commented upon by Miaozong. It was apparently Jiqi Hongchu himself who suggested the title of this collection, *The Concordant Sounds Collection of Verse Commentaries,* a title meant to suggest the extent to which he felt his women disciples Baochi and Zukui were able to "resonate" both poetically and spiritually with each other, with their Song dynasty predecessor Miaozong, and ultimately, with the truth exemplified and embodied by the early great Chan masters themselves.[24]

---

24. One of the earliest uses of the word *hexiang* 合響 (which I have translated as "concordant sounds" but which could also be translated as "singing together in harmony"), can be found

For the most part, I have refrained from supplying my own interpretations to the verses translated in this book. I would, however, like to briefly explore this notion of mutual resonance by looking at the verses composed by Miaozong, Baochi, and Zukui in response to case 41:

> When Fayan heard the fish-drum announcing the meal, he asked a monk if he still heard something. "If just now you heard something, then now you do not. If now you hear something, just now you didn't hear anything."

The main protagonist in this case is the Tang dynasty Chan master Fayan Wenyi 法眼文益 (885–958).[25] Master Fayan appears to be using the notion of hearing and not-hearing to suggest the difference between immediate experience and experience remembered or recalled.

In her verse commentary, Miaozong takes this image of not-hearing and extends it to include not-speaking, and in the last line, plays with the paradoxical fact that Fayan has to speak in order to suggest that which is no longer immediately true once it is spoken or heard.

> The ear listens as if it were deaf;
> The mouth speaks as though mute.
> At the tip of Fayan's tongue:
> What is real, and what is fake?

---

in China's first work of literary criticism, written by Liu Xie (465–522). In a chapter entitled "Literary Talents," Liu characterizes the poets Xi Kang (223–62 CE) and Ruan Ji (210–63 CE) as follows: "Together, these writers compose a symphony of sounds and fly in perfect formation, although each has a unique pair of wings." See Vincent Yu-chung Shih, trans., *The Literary Mind and the Carving of the Dragons: A Study of Thought and Pattern in Chinese Literature* (New York: Columbia University Press, 1959), 255.

25. Albert Welter has noted, the historical Fayan appears to have been a rather conventional Chan Buddhist who criticized some of the "illnesses" of the Chan school, including the cavalier dismissal of traditional teachings, not to mention traditional teaching methods such as using words to explicate and explain. This stands in sharp contrast to the image of the iconoclastic teacher painted in transmission-lamp records such as the *Jingde Transmission of the Lamp*. See Albert Welter, *Monks, Rulers, and Literati: The Political Ascendancy of Chan Buddhism* (New York: Oxford University Press, 2006), 139–44.

Baochi in her verse also features Fayan, although she does not refer to him explicitly by name. She also focuses on the impossibility of capturing the ineffable in words. Unlike Miaozong, however, she does not have Fayan speaking, but rather plucking a flower from the void and floating the moon on the water.

> From the void he plucks a flower;
> In the water, he floats the moon.
> The crime that has filled universe:
> How can one explain it in words?

Flowers that appear in the void (or emptiness) and the moon reflected in the water are, of course, familiar metaphors for the inherently impermanent and illusory reality of forms that manifest or emerge from emptiness. Here, Baochi would seem to be suggesting that Fayan is in fact contributing to his student's confusion by treating both the flowers and the moon's reflection as real by plucking and floating them—thus the accusation of criminal behavior.

While both Miaozong and Baochi use imagery and allusive language, Zukui in her poem prefers to cut to the chase by sending the sounds (of speaking and hearing) and the shapes (flowers and the moon's reflection) back to their source: the "dreams in your head." And in her final line, she returns to the distinction between the time something is experienced and the time it is recalled, by exhorting her readers to go wandering instead in "time-less time." Zukui's verse commentary is as follows:

> A patch of empty substance beyond saying and feeling:
> Who has ever explained the realization of the Unborn?
> Summon back the shapes and sounds to the dreams in your head;
> Roam the timeless-time of the bodhisattva Wonderful Sound.[26]

---

26. The story of the great bodhisattva Gadgadasvara or "Wonderful Sound," appears in Chapter 24 of the *Lotus Sūtra*.

Chan verses such as these are very difficult to fully explicate—indeed they are designed to discourage any kind of definitive explanation. However, perhaps this brief comparison of the three verses may help explain the idea suggested by the title of this collection: three voices sounding in harmony but also distinctively themselves.

This work, as far as I know, is the only such extant collection of female-authored verse commentaries in Chinese. In fact, it would appear to be one of the reasons it was first printed at all: as Zhang Dayuan exclaims in his preface, it is a collection that "elevates womankind and puts to men to shame." In other words, while they may not necessarily reflect a uniquely feminine perspective as such, in composing these verses, Miaozong, Baochi and Zukui were claiming for themselves the same religious and spiritual authority as their male counterparts, no more and no less. Moreover, verse commentaries such as these also served to pay homage to earlier masters in the tradition, much like the tradition of "matching rhymes" in the Chinese secular poetic tradition, whereby a poet would compose a poem using the same rhymes as those of an earlier poet. Thus, the fact that the two seventeenth-century women Chan masters felt moved to follow the example of their twelfth-century female spiritual ancestor points to an awareness and appreciation of a distinctly female lineage within an overwhelmingly patrilineal, if not entirely patriarchal, tradition. In the end, however, what is important is not that these verses are composed by women, but simply that they are worth savoring, whether for their poetic qualities or their spiritual suggestiveness, or both.

The Text of

THE CONCORDANT SOUNDS COLLECTION
OF VERSE COMMENTARIES

Songgu hexiang ji

頌古合響集

Preface by Layman Zhang Dayuan

Vases and trays, bracelets and hairpins, may all be fashioned of gold, but unless they are flung to the ground in order make a sound [to prove that they are indeed gold], they might as well be fashioned of ceramic tile! In the same way, the single earthshaking shout of Mazu's that caused Baizhang to go deaf for three days can be said to be a case of there being a resonance in the words.[27] Linji was able to distinguish the *gong* and *shang* notes and *lü* pitches within a single phrase,[28] and at noon, he beat the drum announcing the third watch [midnight]. After that, the descendants of these masters came up with *sulu xili*.[29] In Guo Xiang's commentary on *Zhuangzi* there is no room for speculation—host and guest are clearly defined.[30] In the butterfly dream of Zhuang Zhou there is no attachment to name, no attachment to form, no need to ask anything of or involve oneself with others. Because the old woman who gave birth to the seven children could not find anyone who understood her, she flung into the river both the

27. Baizhang Huaihai's百丈懷海 (720–814) teacher, the great Mazu, was said to have once let out a loud shout that left his pupil deaf for three days. The analogy being made here seems to be a that a shout, like a vase or a tray, may seem to be nothing more than a shout, until it is used as a "test" between an enlightened master and a ready disciple, at which time it reveals its golden qualities, the special sound or "resonance" within apparently ordinary words or actions.

28. These all refer to the tones and pitches of the traditional Chinese musical scale, which are different from those of Western music.

29. A reference to the exchange between the Song dynasty master Dahui Zonggao and the layman-official, described in the introduction, in which the layman tried to demonstrate understanding but only uttered seemingly nonsensical words. (It is possible that these words were originally a form of mantra or incantation. See Kirchner, 47, n. 2.)

30. See Watson, *The Zen Teachings of Master Lin-Chi*, 19. Guo Xiang, as noted earlier, was the author of an unfinished commentary to the *Zhuangzi*. "Host" (*zhu* 主) and "guest" (*bin* 賓) are terms often used by Linji and later Chan masters to refer to the different "roles" or stances assumed by master and student in order to test understanding. More abstractly, it refers to the "empty" play between noumena and phenomena, subject and object, etc.

moon reflected in the water and the clouds over the mountains.[31] It was not until several hundred years later that we find Miaozong,[32] who was just as spirited and without spending a single penny bought fried-cakes in the village and with a shout emerged from Dahui's hall.[33] She mastered the five notes and so harmonized with them such that when listening to her it was hard to distinguish between hers and those of other enlightened masters.[34] Thus, a single thread connected her with the ancient worthies as she lifted the oars, danced in the waves to a different melody. Up to now, no one has been able to harmonize with Miaozong and Dahui; until the Venerable Jiqi Hongchu of Lingyan appeared and restored Chan to its corrected beginnings, the five hundred years since Dahui's passing have been marked by a confused dissonance.

Among Jiqi's disciples there were two who resonated with Miaozong: one was Person of the Way Baochi from Miaozhan Chan Nunnery; the other was the abbess Zukui from Lingrui Nunnery. Baochi was the daughter of a well-known family who married into the Xu household. Her father-in-law had died a martyr to the fallen Ming dynasty and was posthumously honored with the rank of Chief Minister of the Court of the Imperial Stud; her husband's grandfather had served as Vice-Minister of War. Theirs was a family tradition of loyalty and filial piety. When her esteemed husband unexpectedly died, she began to "sing to a different tune." Feeling revulsion toward worldly affairs, she abandoned them and every day from dawn to dusk studied with the abbess Zukui. She practiced hard and with great determination. One day she happened to be reading

31. A reference to the case raised by Dahui and the poem written by Miaozong composed in response (see the introduction).
32. In this preface, Zhang uses Miaozong's religious name Wuzhuo. In order to avoid confusion, I have replaced this with the name Miaozong.
33. This is an allusion to yet another well-known Dharma encounter between Miaozong and Dahui. It begins with Dahui asking Miaozong, "The men of ancient times did not leave their quarters, so how could they be in the village eating fried cakes?" Miaozong replies, "Only if the master lets me off, will I dare to tell him something." Dahui then says, "I have already let you off, now try saying something!" "I have also let the master off!" retorts Miaozong. Dahui then asks, "What is the point of struggling over fried cakes?" Instead of replying, Miaozong lets out a shout and then another, after which she simply leaves the room.
34. As noted above, the "five notes" refer to the traditional Chinese musical scale. A popular expression used to refer to someone who is tone-deaf or who lacks musical ability is "the five tones are not all there" (*wuyin bu quan* 五音不全).

Jiqi Hongchu of Lingyan's discourse records, and it was as if the warmth of the springtime sun had suddenly penetrated into a wintry valley. She immediately went to ask for an audience with the elderly monk who, as soon as he saw her, saw she had the qualities of a "manly man."

After the death of her husband, Baochi—by now approaching middle age—requested ordination from Master Jiqi Hongchu. She then began to practice together with the community and would request teachings from the elderly master. After every teaching that he gave, she would fiercely apply herself,[35] neglecting to both sleep and eat in her determination to unlock the deepest and mysterious truth of ultimate realization. She would also clap her hands and sing together with the abbess Zukui: they were like two mouths but one without a tongue.[36] The venerable monk assisted them in this and delightedly instructed them so that in the future the lineage would never again sink into obscurity, and so that Miaozong would no longer walk alone. Baochi and Zukui then composed their own verse commentaries using the same rhyme schemes as those used by Miaozong and in so doing plains and rivers were overturned and kicked upside-down and ten thousand boats and ships were chewed to bits. Yan Duolo from Mount Jing[37] after reading them carefully testified that, although these two women collaborated in the writing of these commentaries, they did not borrow from each other; just as within the bell there is no echo of drums, and within the drum there is no sound of bells.[38] When he showed them to the Venerable Master Jiqi for his approval, the master said, "They can be said to exemplify 'concordant sounds' (hexiang)." When he gave them to me to read, I was amazed and could not wait to let everyone know about them since each and every one of them touched on the essence.

35. In other words, she would jab herself painfully with the tip of an awl. Traditionally, scholars were said to prick their thigh with the point of an awl in order to stay awake while studying.
36. This phrase appears in numerous Chan texts. It may possibly be another way of referring to the Chan ideal of an understanding that, while it makes use of words and language, goes beyond words and language: thus, one mouth has a tongue, while the other does not. Here, however, Zhang appears to be simply playing on the notion of two poetic voices expressing a timeless truth that lies beyond poetry, or words.
37. Yan Duluo, also known as Yan Dacan 嚴大參 (1590–1671) was a Buddhist layman and friend of Zhang Dayuan.
38. See the introduction.

Although on the surface it would appear that now anyone with ears can ear it, what is that we call "sounds" (*xiang*)? And even if one understands what sounds are, one must still ask what it means for them to be in unison. To say that they are "in unison" is to be as careless as those who, because the three characters are written in a similar way, take *wu* and *yan* to be *ma*.[39] To say that they are "not in unison" is like saying that one drop is just black ink but that with two drops a dragon is created.[40] Those who intellectually understand this explanation will not have faith in it until from dawn to dusk they themselves have personally experienced it. Rain on the eaves, the water in Yan Creek,[41] the piece of broken tile striking the bamboo;[42] warbling orioles in the willow trees: all of these are "sounds." Old Laywoman Ling's weeping, Old Woman Yu's laughter, the calling out to Little Jade, and the slapping of Zhaozhou—all of these are also "sounds."[43]

39. The Chinese characters *wu* 烏, *yan* 焉, and *ma* 馬 look quite similar, but their meanings are very different. The popular phrase "wu and yan become ma" refers to careless copying or proofreading.

40. Chinese tradition has it that when an artist dots the two eyes of a painted dragon, it comes alive. Here again, the implication may be that it is precisely because these poems are written in collaboration rather than singly that they come alive.

41. This is an allusion to the story of the recently arrived monk who asks the Tang dynasty master Xuansha Shibei 玄沙師備 (830–908) how he should begin his practice. Xuansha replied, "Do you hear the sound of the water in Yan Creek?" When the monk replies that he does, Xuansha says, "That is the place of your entry." *Chan Master Xuansha Shibei's Discourse Records* (*Xuansha Shibei chanshi yulu* 玄沙師備禪師語錄) CBETA X73, 1446: 34c24.

42. One day as Chan Master Xiangyan Zhixian 香嚴智閑 (d. 898) was cutting grass, his scythe struck a piece of broken tile, which flew up and hit a bamboo. When he heard the sound of tile on bamboo, he experienced an awakening. This episode later became a popular kōan. See Kirchner, *Entangling Vines*, 49.

43. Old Laywoman Ling, who is said to have emerged victorious from a Dharma battle with Fubei 浮盃, a disciple of the famous Tang master Mazu, at one point responds to Fubei's words by exclaiming, with tears in her eyes, that "Yet another wrong has been added to the blue sky." Old Woman Yu is said to have had an experience of awakening while she was on the street selling her cakes and heard a beggar singing. "Calling Little Jade" refers to a popular poem about a young woman who calls out to her servant Little Jade so that the man she loves, but cannot talk too, will hear her voice. Yuanwu Keqin (who would later compile *The Blue Cliff Record*) is said to have attained enlightenment when his teacher, Wuzu Fayan 五祖法演 (1024–1104), asked him whether or not he was familiar with this poem. There are several well-known stories about Zhaozhou's encounters with old women. In the one referred to here, Zhaozhou meets a woman carrying a basket of bamboo shoots, which, she tells him, she is taking to Zhaozhou. When he asks her what she would do if she were to unexpectedly run into the master, she just gives him a good slap. These stories are also

Deshan's blows, Linji's shouts, the striking of the gatepost, the three catties of hemp are also "sounds."[44] These sounds can awaken all of the people in the world; they also can deafen all the people of the world. If awakened, then without even a single additional sentence, they will be able to transcend a hundred million. If deafened, then the text that follows will be too long, and even with these writings and texts, they will descend into confusion and even five years will not suffice to explain it.[45] If today there is anyone who can resonate with the distinctive tune of Zhuang Zhou's dream,[46] I would ask them to take these sounds and post them so that people walking along the busy streets will hear them even if they think it is coming from the east, although it is actually coming from the west. In this way, even if the students of the world do not want to listen to these sounds, they will hear them and die [to the delusions of the world].[47] And even

---

well-known kōans. Here, however, they are being used primarily as examples of different sorts of sounds that, under the right conditions, can trigger an experience of awakening.

44. The great Chan master Deshan Xuanjian 德山宣鑑 (782–865) was known for his effective pedagogical use of blows and Linji was known for his use of shouts. The reference to the gatepost may refer to the story of Linji who once pointed to a wooden gatepost and asked whether it was a ordinary human or a sage. When he did not receive a reply, he hit the gatepost and said, "Even if you had come up with an answer, it would still be nothing more than a wooden post!" In case 12 of *The Blue Cliff Record*, when Chan Master Dongshan Liangjie 洞山良价 (807–69) is asked what a buddha is, he replies "three catties of hemp." A cattie is unit of weight equivalent to 500 grams.

45. Once when Master Yunmen was asked what he was going to talk about, he replied "The text that follows is too long. Let's postpone it to another day!" Urs App, *Master Yunmen: From the Record of the Chan Master "Gate of the Clouds"* (New York: Kodansha International, 1994), 114. In case 58 of *The Blue Cliff Record*, we find Master Zhaozhou replying to a query by a monk as follows: "Once someone asked me, and for five years, I really couldn't explain it." *Chan Master Foguo Yuanwu's Blue Cliff Record (Foguo Yuanwu Chanshi Biyan lu* 佛果圓悟禪師碧巖錄) CBETA T48, 2003: 191c9.

46. In the original text, what I have translated as "harmony" is indicated by the names of the first two notes of the traditional Chinese musical scale; as a compound, it is often used to refer generally to music or harmony—the implication being that it takes more than one note to create music.

47. What is meant here is that anyone who hears (or reads) these poems will find their defilements destroyed—in other words, it is the defilements that will die. These lines are based on the following passage in Chapter 9 of the *Great Nirvana Sūtra (Mahāparanirvāna-Sūtra*): "Imagine a man who painted a great drum with a medicine made up of a mixture of poisons. When he pounded that drum in a crowd, even those with no inclination to listen would nevertheless hear it, and all who did would die. But there would be one exception: a person who did not die unexpectedly from this. This Mahāyāna scripture, the *Great Nirvana Sūtra* is like that. It produces an audible sound everywhere, and those living beings

when those among them who have committed the four major transgressions[48] and have fallen into the Avici Hell,[49] hear these sounds, they will also indirectly give rise to the supreme awakening. How is this different from coming to the aid of the orphaned and those in distress and persuading people to be kind and warm? This collection elevates womankind and puts to men[50] to shame.

---

that do hear it will find their greed, anger, and stupidity completely destroyed. Among them there will even be some who do not otherwise think about these things yet will notice that the causal power of the *Great Nirvana [Sūtra]* has destroyed their defilements, and their fetters have disappeared by themselves. And when it comes to those who have transgressed by committing one of the four serious offenses or five heinous crimes, upon hearing the sūtra they, too, will create the causal conditions that lead to the highest bodhi, gradually losing their defilements . . ." (T12n0374 *Dabanniepan jing* 9:420). See Mark L. Blum, trans., *The Nirvana Sūtra (Mahāparanirvāna-Sūtra) BDK English Tripitaka Series. (Berkeley, CA: Bukkyo Dendo Kyokai America, Inc., 2013), 291.

48. The four major transgressions for monks are killing, stealing, sexual activity, and lying about one's spiritual attainments.

49. The deepest and most long lasting of the Buddhist hells. Here Zhang does not use the term Avici but rather a description of this hell as a place where five things continue without interval or respite, including suffering, time, and karma and its consequences.

50. Literally, those with "beards and whiskers."

鉼盤釵釧鎔作一金，若非擲地出聲，與瓦礫何異。所以馬祖震威一喝，百丈三日耳聾，袛為言中有響。臨濟向一句內別出宮商律呂翻成，日午打三更。從此遞代兒孫蘇嚧嗓哩。莊子註郭象未容擬議，主賓分。蝴蝶夢莊周，離相離名，人不稟帶累。婆生七子不遇知音，水月雲山一時拋卻。數百年後方得無著與他出氣，不費一文錢買箇庄上油餈。一喝便出大慧堂中。直得五音並奏二聽難聞，遂將從上古德一串穿。卻呈橈舞棹別宮商，至今無人和得。大慧沒五百年繁音雜，與靈喦老人出而還之正始。座下繼響無著者兩人，一則籹湛總道人，一則靈瑞符菴主也。道人名家子，適徐門。其翁殉節，隨州贈太僕卿。祖翁為少司馬家傳忠孝。忽焉大雅云亡，風吹別調，厭棄世相。晨夕同符菴主苦志力參。一日讀靈喦錄，如寒谷忽遇陽春，亟趨參請老人。一見以大丈夫目之。夫亡畢葬即，詣山剃染受具足戒。隨眾參請老人。每令下語痛加錐劄，寢食俱廢，驀地撥著向上關捩。與符菴主唱拍相隨，兩口無一舌。老人為之助，喜囑令加護嗣後不復，肯遜無著獨步，取其頌古和之。踏翻平江萬斛舟嚼碎。徑山輥轆鑽，即兩人亦各各不相借，鐘中無鼓響，鼓中無鐘聲，共以質老人，老人曰，此可稱合響矣。大圓讀之大驚。不待供通知。其各各詣實也。雖然面目現在有耳共聞，喚甚麼作響，直饒會得響，更問甚處是他合處。若道是合，則字經三寫烏焉成馬，若道不合，則一點水墨兩處成龍。知其解者，旦暮遇之方信。簷前雨，偃溪水，瓦礫擊竹，柳上啼鶯，總是這箇響。凌行哭，俞婆笑，呼小玉，掌趙州，也是這箇響。德山棒，臨濟喝，乾矢橛，麻三斤，也是這箇響。此響亦能悟卻天下人，亦能聾卻天下人。悟則佛法無多一句了然超百億，聾則向下文長，直得五年分疏不下，即今還有向蝴蝶夢中別得宮商者麼。請以此響懸之通衢一任諸人東考西擊，使天下學者雖無心欲聞聞之皆死，其中即有犯四重禁及五無間聞是響，已亦作無上菩提遠因。豈啻扶孤危而摧軟煖。愧鬚眉而冠巾幗也哉。

The Cases and Verses

CASE 1
The World-Honored One Ascends the Seat

One day, the World-Honored One ascended the seat. When the great assembly had gathered and settled down, Mañjuśrī struck his gavel and said, "Observe deeply the Dharma of the Dharma King; the Dharma of the Dharma King is like this." The World-Honored One then came down from the seat.[51]

世尊一日陞座。 大眾纔集定。 文殊白槌云， 諦觀法王法，法王法如是。
世尊便下座。

CHAN MASTER MIAOZONG[52]

The true teaching has been transmitted in its entirety;
No method, worldly or sacred, has been kept hidden.
The prison gates shatter into a hundred bits and pieces:
The brilliance of flinty spark and lightning flash!

正令付全提
不存凡聖機
牢關百雜碎
石火電光輝

51. With a very few minor exceptions, the versions of the cases in this collection are the same as those found in Puhui's thirteenth-century anthology *The Comprehensive String of Pearls Collection of Praise Verses from the Chan School* where Miaozong's original verses are found. Many of these cases are now quite well known; however I have noted only those that appear in *The Blue Cliff Record*, Thomas Cleary's translation, since this collection was in circulation during Miaozong's lifetime. I have not made reference to collections such as *The Gateless Gate* (*Wumen guan*), which appeared after Miaozong's death, and to which she would not have had access.
52. In the original text, the headings are Wuzhuo, Miaozhan, and Lingrui respectively. To avoid confusion, I have used the names Miaozong, Baochi and Zukui.

Chan Master Baochi

A single eyelash in your eye—falling sky-flowers;[53]
A single sound in your ear—poison-smeared drum.[54]
If you busy yourself with worries, you will never understand
How beneath the gavel, the bitter is separated from the sweet.

一翳在眼空花墮
一聲入耳塗毒鼓
百萬忙忙總不知
卻來椎下分甘苦

Chan Master Zukui

A lightning-like stratagem that confuses both men and gods;
A single blow smashes it to bits, suffusing the world with light.
Great wisdom can seem foolish; great skill can seem clumsy,[55]
And even Gautama had to learn how to train his unruly mind!

The elephant's carriage proceeds along the road with slow dignity—
How could a praying mantis even think of stopping its advance![56]
In front of a crowd of hundreds, his lips curved up in a smile,
He conveys the teaching directly without lodging it in words.

53. An eyelash in the eye can distort the vision: sky flowers (*kong hua* 空華, or "flowers in the sky") refers to the spots that appear in the eye when you press your finger against the eyelids. Since the character "kong" also means emptiness, this compound can also be translated as "flowers of emptiness" and as such refer to the illusory nature of what we ordinarily take to be substantial and real.
54. See note 47 above.
55. The original source for this phrase is the Daoist classic *Tao Te Ching*, chapter 47.
56. These two lines are from the "Song of Realizing the Way" ("Dengdao ge 證道歌"), often translated as "Song of Enlightenment," by Chan Master Yongjia Xuanjue 永嘉玄覺 (665–713). The elephant is used to symbolize the great bodhisattva who steadily advances along the path, unswayed by those of inferior insight who attempt to deflect him from his goal. This may be indirectly alluding to a passage from chapter 4 of the *Zhuangzi*: "Don't you know about the praying mantis? Angrily waving its arms, it blocks the path of an onrushing chariot, not realizing that the task is far beyond it." See Burton Watson, trans., *The Complete Works of Zhuangzi* (New York: Columbia University Press, 2013), 90.

掣電之機人天罔知
一椎粉碎遍界流輝
大智若愚大巧若拙
潦倒瞿曇狂心未歇

象駕崢嶸漫進途
誰信螳蜋能拒轍
百眾人前口似眉
有理直教無處說

CASE 2
A Non-Buddhist Achieves Realization

A non-Buddhist asked the World-Honored One, "I do not ask about that which has words; I do not ask about that which is wordless." The World-Honored One just sat there. The non-Buddhist praised him, saying, "The World-Honored One has compassionately dispelled the clouds of confusion and made it possible for me to gain entry." He then paid obeisance and left. Afterward, Ananda asked the Buddha, "What did the non-Buddhist realize, so that he was able to say that he had gained entry?" The World-Honored One said, "He was like a fine steed who runs as soon as he sees the shadow of the whip."[57]

世尊因外道問云，不問有言不問無言。 世尊據坐。 外道讚曰，世尊大慈開我
迷雲令我得入， 乃便作禮而去。 後阿難問佛，外道有何所證，而言得入。
世尊曰， 如世良馬見鞭影而行。

CHAN MASTER MIAOZONG

By means of the tiger-trapping stratagem, both sides are settled;
Once the torrential flow is cut off, all the myriad sources dry up.
The fine steed only needs a glimpse of the shadow of the whip;
His hooves meant for frost and chill, his fur for the freezing cold.[58]

---

57. See *The Blue Cliff Record*, case 65. In the *Saṃyuktāgama Sūtra* (*Za ahan jing*) the Buddha speaks of four different kinds of horses. The finest of these will run in the desired direction at the mere shadow of the whip, the second best begins to run just before the whip reaches his flesh, and the third best runs as soon as it feels the pain of the whip on its body. The worst horse, however, does not run until the pain has penetrated to the marrow of its bones. CBETA T2, 99: 233b15–16.
58. An allusion to the chapter of the *Zhuangzi* entitled "Horse Hoofs," which begins, in the translation by Burton Watson, "Horses' hoofs are made for treading frost and snow, their coats for keeping out wind and cold. To munch grass, drink from the stream, lift up their

陷虎機關兩處安
湍流一截萬源乾
駿駒瞥爾窺鞭影
凜凜霜蹄毛骨寒

CHAN MASTER BAOCHI

The non-Buddhist hammers down a stake in the hollow void,
Rejoicing that yet another mote has been thrown in the eyes.
The Old Barbarian conveyed the transmission in its entirety
And yet he still managed to mistake a tortoise for a sea-turtle!

外道虛空釘橛
慶喜眼中添屑
老胡據令全提
難免證龜成鱉

CHAN MASTER ZUKUI

Frosty hooves prance about in the shadow of the whip
And kick up the fallen red flowers in the spring breeze.
Once the gates of mystery have been shattered into bits,
Nowhere in the numberless worlds will there be a trace.

掇轉霜蹄鞭影中
春風蹴踏落花紅
一從擊碎玄關後
剎剎塵塵不見蹤

---

feet and gallop—this is the true nature of horses. Though they might possess great terraces and fine halls, they would have not use for them." See Burton Watson, *The Complete Works of Zhuangzi* (New York: Columbia University Press, 2013), 104.

CASE 3
A Woman Comes Out of Samadhi

When Mañjuśrī was on Spirit Peak where all of the buddhas were gathered, he saw a woman who had entered into samadhi sitting close to the seat of the Buddha. Mañjuśrī asked the Buddha, "Why is it this woman gets to sit near the Buddha's seat?" The Buddha replied, "If you want to know, why don't you bring this woman out of her samadhi and ask her?" Mañjuśrī circled the woman three times, snapped his fingers once, and took her to the Brahma realm. But although he exhausted all of his magical powers, he was unable to bring her out.

The Buddha said, "Even a hundred thousand Mañjuśrīs would be unable to bring this woman out of her samadhi. However, below us, past forty-two realms as numerous as the sands of the Ganges, there is the Bodhisattva Not-Clear[59] who can bring this woman out of samadhi." In an instant, the Bodhisattva Not-Clear had appeared there where the Buddha was, and the Buddha ordered him to bring the woman out of her samadhi. The Bodhisattva Not-Clear stood in front of the woman and snapped his fingers once, at which the woman came out of samadhi.

文殊師利在靈山會上 諸佛集處，見一女子近佛坐入於三昧。 文殊白佛云，何此女得近佛坐。 佛云，汝但覺此女令從三昧起，汝自問之。 文殊繞女子三匝，鳴指一下。 乃至托上梵天。 盡其神力而不能出。 佛云，假使百千文殊，亦出此女定不得。 下方過四十二恒沙國土，有罔明菩薩能出此女定。 須臾罔明至佛所。 佛敕出此女定。 罔明即於女子前鳴指一下。 女子於是從定而出。

---

59. The Bodhisattva Not-Clear is a bodhisattva at a level lower than Mañjuśrī, who is generally regarded as the bodhisattva of perfect enlightenment. Here however, it is he rather than Mañjuśrī who succeeds in bringing the girl out of her trance.

Chan Master Miaozong

Gold is not bartered for gold;
Nor water washed with water.
There is no Two to be transformed into One;
How can there be a Not-Clear and a Mañjuśrī?
How can one scratch through one's boot soles![60]

金不博金
水不洗水
兩既不成
一何有爾
罔明文殊
靴裏動指

Chan Master Baochi

Once in samadhi, what need to talk about how spring follows autumn?
Doubt rises, emotion stirs, distinctions are made between far and near.
Before long the Sun God of the East will have exhausted all his powers
In a vain attempt to get the precious peony flower to open up for him![61]

一定那論秋復春
疑生情動見疏親
等閒廢盡東君力
空使名花解笑人

60. This translation is tentative; I am reading it as a possible variant of the popular Chinese saying "To scratch an itch with one's boots on," which means to do something ineffectively.
61. The name Dongjun 東君 or "Lord of the East," appears in texts dating back at least to the second century BCE and may have originally been the name of a solar deity.

Chan Master Zukui

Everyone possesses his own parcel of vacant land,[62]
So who would dare make even the slightest error?
The girl and Not-Clear and Mañjuśrī:
With a single verdict all are declared guilty!

人人有片閑田
誰敢絲毫錯誤
女子网明文殊
總與一狀領過

---

62. In Chan Buddhist texts, a vacant plot of land often refers to the pure and untainted mind.

CASE 4
Aṅgulimāla and the Difficult Delivery

After Aṅgulimāla had left the householder's life and become a monk, he went into the city with his begging bowl. He came to the home of a wealthy man whose wife was having a difficult delivery. The man said, "As a disciple of Gautama, you must be very wise. Is there not something you can do to spare my wife this difficult delivery?" Aṅgulimāla replied, "I have only recently entered the way, and do not yet know any way of doing this. I will go and ask the Buddha and then return and tell you." And so he returned and explained the matter to the Buddha who then told him, "Go quickly and say to him, 'In all the time I have followed the saintly and sagely Way, never once have I taken life.'" Aṅgulimāla went back and told the wealthy man. As soon as his wife heard this, she gave birth; both mother and child were fine.[63]

殃崛摩羅既出家為沙門，因持缽入城至一長者家，值其婦產難，子母未分。長者云，瞿曇弟子汝為至聖，當有何法能免產難。殃崛曰，我乍入道未知此法，當去問佛卻來相報。遽返白佛，具陳上事，佛告曰，汝速去報言，我自從賢聖法來未曾殺生。殃崛往告。其婦聞知當時分娩，母子平安。

---

63. According to tradition, Aṅgulimāla was a notorious murderer who had killed 999 people, stringing a finger from each victim in a garland around his neck ("Aṅgulimāla" means "garland of fingers") before he was converted by the Buddha and entered the path. It is interesting to speculate why, of the many episodes from Aṅgulimāla's life, this one became a kōan. The statement made by the reformed murderer that he has never killed a single being—which is what Buddha instructs Aṅgulimāla to tell the woman suffering the pains of a difficult birth—can be understood as meaning that he himself has been "reborn" into the Dharma.

Chan Master Miaozong

Neither slow by a single step,
Nor quick by a single minute.
The clear-eyed patch-robed monk:
How does he know what to do?
Shattered bones and crushed flesh won't cancel your debts;
One word of insight is worth ten million words of apology.

不遲一步
不疾一刻
明眼衲僧
如何會得
粉骨碎身未足酬
一句了然超百億

Chan Master Baochi

A tree overgrown with weeds, a jade carved to perfection;
A lonely and desolate spot, a view of elegance and charm.
The young lad seeking out the source of the night fragrance
Sees nothing but the moon shining at the foot of the stairs.

一樹蘢蔥玉刻成
飄廊點地色輕盈
兒童夜覓香來處
惟見階前碎月明

CHAN MASTER ZUKUI

Smash and break open the fetters of gold;[64]
Lift and flip over the platter of white jade.[65]
Others may be concerned over loss and gain,
But nothing can touch one's peace of mind.

敲斷黃金鎖
掀翻白玉盤
他家門得失
莫向寸心安

64. The gold fetters refer to the "chains" of the *vinaya*, or monastic regulations, which are useful but not something to become attached to. In other contexts, they may also refer to attachments to family and children.
65. A platter or disc of white jade is often used in Chinese poetry as a metaphor for the full moon.

CASE 5
The Mind That Emerges from the Empty Void

The *Śūraṅgama Sūtra* says, "You should know that your mind, which emerges from the empty void, is like a lone cloud dotting the clear expanse of sky. How much more so is this true of all of the many worlds within that empty void? Should even a single one of you realize the truth and return to the source, then the emptiness of the ten directions will be completely obliterated."

楞嚴經，當知虛空生汝心內，猶如片雲點太清裏。況諸世界在虛空耶。汝等一人發真歸元，此十方空皆悉消殞。

CHAN MASTER MIAOZONG

When one person discovers the truth and returns to the source,
The great emptiness of the ten directions is completely obliterated.
May I ask about "Yangqi's prickly chestnut"—
How is it like "Yunmen's sesame flatcakes"?[66]

一人發真歸元
十方虛空消殞
試問楊岐栗蓬
何似雲門胡餅

66. Yangqi's prickly chestnut is a metaphor found in many Chan sources, although not in any of the texts attributed to Yangqi Fanghui 楊岐方會 (992–1049) himself. The sweet meat of the chestnut is protected by spiny covering that makes it difficult to swallow; it is often used as a metaphor for the kōan or for kōan practice. Yunmen's "sesame flatcakes" is said to be the reply given by the Song dynasty Master Yunmen Wenyan 雲門文偃 (864–949) to the question "What is talk that goes beyond buddhas and patriarchs?"

CHAN MASTER BAOCHI

This fellow with belly and guts twisted round like this;
I am not sure how his kindness can ever be fully repaid.
Through the night the great blast of west wind was so fierce,
Even the myriad forms of the universe were scared to death!

倒腹傾腸舉似君
不知若箇解酬恩
祇桓一夜西風惡
萬象森羅盡喪魂

CHAN MASTER ZUKUI

The yellow elm tree at the corner of the house
Has stood there for who knows how many years.
This morning the winds whipped up a storm,
Leaving the ground strewn with coins of gold.[67]

屋角黃榆樹
多來不記年
今朝風信急
滿地是金錢

67. In Chinese literature, yellow leaves on the ground are commonly compared to gold coins.

CASE 6
Mañjuśrī Asks Vimalakīrti about Nonduality

The *Vimalakīrti Sūtra* recounts how the thirty bodhisattvas each discoursed on the gate of nonduality. When it came to Mañjuśrī, he said, "My understanding is that in all of the dharmas, there are no words, no speech, no teaching, and no knowledge, and that to separate oneself from all questions and answers is the way by which bodhisattvas enter the gate of nonduality." Mañjuśrī asked Vimalakīrti about this, but Vimalakīrti remained silent. Mañjuśrī sighed and said, "This is the ultimate in wordlessness and letters; this is the true entry into the gate of nonduality. When he spoke of the entry into the gate of the nonduality, five thousand bodhisattvas all entered the gate of nonduality and achieved the deathless Dharma patience."

維摩經，三十二菩薩各說不二法門。至文殊云我於一切法無言無說無示無識離諸問答是為菩薩入不二法門。殊問維摩摩默然。殊歎曰，乃至無有語言文字是真入不二法門。說是入不二法門時，與此眾中五千菩薩皆入不二法門，得無生法忍。

CHAN MASTER MIAOZONG

The old master of Vaiśālī[68] was skilled at concealing his methods;
The thundering sound of his silence penetrated the four directions.
Present and past they all vied to convey the truth of nonduality
But were in fact like children placated by coins of yellow leaves.[69]

---

68. Vaiśālī was the name of Vimalakīrti's hometown.
69. The parents who show a weeping child the golden leaves from the tree saying that they are golden coins are likened to the skillful buddhas who deter sentient beings from their evildoing with descriptions of the joys and pleasures of the upper thirty-three deva realms. This analogy is found in many Chan writings.

毘耶老子善藏機
淵默雷聲徹四維
今古兢傳真不二
豈知黃葉止兒啼

Chan Master Baochi

Vimalakīrti taught by manifesting the silence that is not silence;
The confused Mañjuśrī's achievement was no achievement at all.
The white sun in the blue sky grabs the fire and runs off with it;[70]
Make the slightest distinction—a thief stealing in broad daylight![71]

維摩示現默非默
潦倒文殊得非得
白日青天把火行
分明一夥白拈賊

Chan Master Zukui

The mountain is naturally tall, the water naturally deep;
Don't use the jasper lute to express what is petty and trite.
At the height of spring, the white snow twirls and swirls;
Don't fiddle with the *gong* and *shang* of this melody![72]

山自高兮水自深
漫將瑣瑣寄瑤琴
陽春白雪都翻轉
別整宮商一段音

70. White sun in a blue sky refers to a perfectly clear day—a mind without any clouds of deluded thoughts or mental discriminations.
71. In Chan language, the "thief" can have a variety of meanings; in some cases it is used to describe the activity of a Chan kōan or the skillful means of a Chan master, both of which stealthily get rid of delusion.
72. The terms *gong* 宮 and *shang* 商 refer to the first two notes of the traditional Chinese five-tone musical scale. Here the suggestion could be that there is no need to fiddle with the natural expression of Buddha nature.

CASE 7
A Monk Asks Dongshan about Nirvana

A monk asked Dongshan Daoquan,[73] "'A servant at the monastery does not enter nirvana, and a bhikkhu who has broken the precepts does not enter hell': what is that all about?" Dongshan replied, "When one is completely liberated, there is no shadow left over. Then one can leap over into nirvana."

僧問洞山詮，清淨行者不入涅槃，破戒比丘不入地獄。時如何。山云度盡無遺影，還他越涅槃。

CHAN MASTER MIAOZONG

The stone statue of Jiazhou,
The iron ox of Xianfu.[74]
When the people are at peace,
They do not complain.
When the rivers are at peace,
They cease to flow.

---

73. Dongshan Daoquan 洞山道詮 was a student of the great master Dongshan Liangjie 洞山良价 (807–69) and is traditionally regarded as the first patriarch of the Caodong 曹洞 (Sōtō in Japanese) school of Chan. This exchange can be found in many Chan sources, including Dongshan Daoquan's brief biographical notice in the *Jingde Transmission of the Lamp*. See CBETA T 51, 2076: 337a27–28.

74. "The stone statue of Jiazhou" refers to the giant buddha of Leshan, construction of which began in 713 and did not end until 803, located along one of the Three Gorges of the Yangzi River overlooking Jiazhou (present-day Sichuan province). Carved into the mountainside, it is still a major tourist attraction today. The "iron ox" refers to a statue of the guardian deity of the Yellow River said to have been built by the legendary King Yu in an effort to control the river's flooding. Legend has it that the statue was so large that its head was in Henan and its tail in Hebei.

嘉州石像
陝府鐵牛
人平不語
水平不流

CHAN MASTER BAOCHI

Pure and spotless, pure and spotless;
Breakers of precepts, breaker of precepts!
It makes one laugh, it makes one grieve;
Which one is true and which one false?
When the water rises, the boat lifts as well;
Where clay is plentiful, the Buddha statue is huge!
The vast Original Thusness is no different from Emptiness;
The wind follows the tiger; the clouds follow the dragon.[75]

清淨清淨
破戒破戒
堪笑堪悲
孰真孰假
水漲船高
泥多佛大
廓然本體等虛空
風從虎兮雲從龍

75. The original source of this phrase is the *I Ching* or *Book of Changes*: "Things with the same tonality resonate together; things with the same material force seek out one another. Water flows to where it is wet; fire goes towards where it is dry. Clouds follow the dragon; winds follow the tiger. . . ." Translation by Richard Lynn, *The Classic of Changes: A New Translation of the* I Ching *as Interpreted by Wang Bi* (New York: Columbia University Press, 1994), 137.

CHAN MASTER ZUKUI

In a forest of thorny brambles, strolling in comfortable ease;
Outside under the bright moon, hiding oneself quietly away.[76]
The spring breezes tug at the blossoms, leaving them in tatters,
And adding to the dust already piled up on Caoxi's mirror.[77]

荊棘林中容坦步
月明簾外闇抽身
春風拽轉花狼籍
添得曹溪鏡裏塵

76. A realized person is able to stroll at ease among the thorns and to live in seclusion even under the bright light of the moon—that is, in a public setting.

77. The home monastery of Huineng 慧能 (638–713), traditionally referred to as the Sixth Patriarch of Chan, was Caoxi 曹溪, located in Guangdong province. The mirror, of course, is an allusion to the famous story in the *Platform Sūtra* about the head monk Shenxiu 神秀 (606?–706) who wrote a poem on the wall in which he compared the mind to a mirror that had to be kept clean of accumulated dust (the so-called gradual method of cultivation). Huineng, who at the time was just an illiterate southerner staying at the monastery, got someone to pen a poem in response, in which he questions the very existence of both mind and dust.

CASE 8
The World-Honored One Holds Up a Flower

The First Indian Patriarch, the Venerable Mahākāśyapa, saw the World-Honored One at the assembly on Vulture Peak hold up a flower and then with his eyes like blue lotuses look around at the great assembly of one hundred thousand sages and saints, but only Kāśyapa broke into a slight smile. The World-Honored One then spoke: "I have the Treasury of the True Dharma Eye, the Marvelous Mind of Nirvana, the True Form of the Formless, and the Subtle Dharma Gate of Liberation, which I am entrusting to you. You must take care that it is transmitted and never allowed to be cut off."[78]

西天初祖摩訶迦葉尊者見世尊在靈山會上拈起一枝華，以青蓮目普視大眾百萬聖賢。惟迦葉破顏微笑。世尊乃曰，吾有正法眼藏，涅槃玅心，實相無相，微玅解脫法門，付囑於汝。汝當護持流通無.

CHAN MASTER MIAOZONG

The iron cangue around his neck weighs three hundred catties;[79]
Clearly distinguished and understood but not easily carried out.

---

78. This, of course, is a version of the famous story of the origin of Chan, the wordless teaching.
79. This may be a reference to the story of Yunmen Wenyan 雲門文偃 (864–949), who was sent by his first teacher, Muzhou Daoming 睦州道明 (780–877), to visit Xuefeng Yicun 雪峰義存 (822–908). On his way there, he met a monk who was also going to visit Xuefeng. Yunmen asked the monk to ask Xuefeng a question on his behalf, but not to tell him that it was from someone else. The monk did as he was told, but when Xuefeng heard the question—"There's an iron cangue on this old fellow's head. Why not remove it?"—he threatened to have the monk beaten. The monk then confessed that that it was not his question, but rather that of a monk he had met in the village. Xuefeng than sent everyone to welcome Yunmen, predicting that he would one day become a great master with hundreds of disciples. See *Compendium of Five Lamps* (*Wudeng huiyuan* 五燈會元) CBETA X 80, 1565: 303b12–17.

With a somber face and skinny legs he sits in front of the peak,
As once again the golden robe[80] deceives those who follow after.

項上鐵枷三百斤
分明有理不容伸
默然雞足峰前坐
猶把金襴詒後人

CHAN MASTER BAOCHI

Holding up a flower, he generously illustrated the truth,
Causing just this one ascetic adept to break into a smile.
The romances of millennia, the resentments of the ages:
With all of these, right and wrong come into the world.

拈花綽約露真詮
引得頭陀獨破顏
千古風流千古恨
是非從此落人間

CHAN MASTER ZUKUI

Spring is filled with white blossoms everywhere one turns,
But to frivolously hold one up would be to lie and deceive.
Even though his smile reveals the nose you were born with,
Before you know it your whole body will fall into the net!

春滿百花無避處
等閒舉起便淆訛
縱然笑豁娘生鼻
不覺全身墮網羅

---

80. It is said that Mahāprajāpatī, the Buddha's foster-mother (and founder of the female monastic order), wove a robe of golden threads for the Buddha, but he did not want to wear it. He tried to pass it on to his disciples, but in the end only the bodhisattva Maitreya was willing to assume it. See John Strong, *Relics of the Buddha* (Motilal Banarsidass, 2007), 217, for a discussion of this and other versions of the story.

CASE 9
Bodhidharma's Sandal

Three years after Great Teacher Bodhidharma was buried on Bear Ear Mountain, Song Yun of Wei, on his return from an official mission to the western regions, ran into the Patriarch in the Congling mountains, carrying one of his sandals in his hands, traveling along alone. When Yun asked him where he was going, the Patriarch replied that he was going to the Western Land [of India]. He also informed Song Yun: "Your master has already become weary of the world." When Song Yun heard this, he hurriedly took his leave from the Patriarch and headed east. By the time he had returned to report on his mission, the Emperor Ming had already passed away. Later when Bodhidharma's grave was opened, nothing was found but an empty coffin with a single sandal inside. The entire court was surprised and delighted, and the remaining sandal was ordered to be placed in the Shaolin Temple and venerated.[81]

達磨大師既葬熊耳山，後三歲，魏宋雲使西域回遇祖於蔥嶺，手攜隻履翩翩獨逝。雲問，師何往。祖曰，西天去。又謂雲曰，汝主已厭世。雲聞之，茫然別祖東。邁暨復命則明帝已登遐矣。迨啟壙惟空棺一隻革履存焉。舉朝為之驚歎，奉詔取遺履於少林寺供養。

CHAN MASTER MIAOZONG

Navigating the sea, he came east on a sliver of bamboo reed,
And on behalf of the Dharma saved others by assuming their heavy
  karma and refuting the king of Liang.
The master had the principle, he taught with immediacy and
  without boundary

---

81. See also *The Blue Cliff Record*, case 1.

In the snow, with his single sandal he returned home to the West,
Through the endless peaks of the Congling mountains.
Upright and dignified, with or without defilements,[82]
If you try to be clever, you will end up the fool.

航海東來點兒落節
為法求人自作深孽
賴遇梁王是作家
有理直教無處雪
及乎隻履復西歸蔥嶺
無端重漏泄不漏泄
分明弄巧反成拙

CHAN MASTER BAOCHI

Successfully looking for people, he would not relinquish his goal;
On a sliver of reed he traveled along the autumnal rivers of Chu.[83]
And now, carrying his single sandal, to where has he returned?
Ten thousand valleys and a thousand streams flow beneath his feet.

得得求人志不休
一葦踏遍楚江秋
而今隻履歸何處
萬壑千溪腳下流

CHAN MASTER ZUKUI

In the beginning the mallet smashed two of his teeth,
Then afterward, he was left with but a single tattered sandal.

82. The word translated here as "defilement" is "leaking" (*āsrava*), which generally speaking refers to a mind that is "tainted" (or not, as the case may be) by delusion and desire.
83. Another popular legend regarding Bodhidharma has him leaving Emperor Wu (who has failed to understand the Indian monk's enigmatic statements) and miraculously crossing the Yangzi River on a reed. According to the legend, he finally settled down at Shaolin Monastery on Mount Song, which is located in Henan Province (in the region traditionally known as Chu).

Full of self-pity, and wanting to split his flesh and shatter his bones,
On that morning he dug a hole and buried himself even more deeply,
So as to make sure that the green maggots wouldn't be able to get in.

最初椎落雙齒末
後狼籍隻履中間
幸自可憐強欲分皮析髓
今朝掘地更深埋免得青

CASE 10
Bodhidharma Pacifies Huike's Mind

When the Second Patriarch, Great Master Huike, first went to Shaolin to seek instruction from Bodhidharma, he stood in the snow, chopped off his arm, wept piteously, and begged for the Dharma. Bodhidharma, knowing that Huike was a Dharma vessel, then said to him, "All of the buddhas when they first sought for instruction about the way, forgot their physical selves for the sake of the Dharma. Today since you have chopped off your arm, I will accept your request." The Patriarch said, "May I hear the Dharma seal of all of the buddhas?" Bodhidharma said, "The Dharma seal of all the buddhas was not received from someone else." The Patriarch said, "My mind is not yet at peace, I beg the master to pacify it for me." Bodhidharma said to him, "Bring your mind here and I will pacify it for you." The Patriarch said, "When I look for my mind, I am unable to find it!" Bodhidharma said, "Your mind has now been pacified." At this, the Patriarch entered the state of enlightenment.

二祖慧可大師初至少林參承達磨，立雪斷臂悲淚求法。磨知是法器乃曰，諸佛最初求道為法忘形，汝今斷臂求亦可在。祖曰諸佛法印可得聞乎。磨曰，諸佛法印不從人得。祖曰我心未寧乞師與安。磨曰，將心來與汝安。祖曰，覓心了不可得。磨曰，與汝安心竟。祖於此悟入。

CHAN MASTER MIAOZONG

Bodhidharma sat for nine years facing the wall,
Until in the middle of the deep snow he got it.
And when he'd got it the myriad forms and
Ten thousand appearances split right in two!

達磨九年面壁坐
深雪之中得一箇

得一箇森羅
萬象平分破

CHAN MASTER BAOCHI

Hoary cliffs ten thousand feet high, snow up to the waist,
The nostrils his mother gave him turn black with frostbite.
He tried out all kinds of tricks but exhausted his cunning,
And this time found it hard to grasp even a strand of hair!

蒼崖萬仞雪齊腰
凍得娘生鼻孔焦
弄出多般窮伎倆
此時難著一絲毫

CHAN MASTER ZUKUI

He was able to get his mind pacified, but his wrist was severed,
Thinking about it makes one want to cry out to the high heavens.
The wind is high, the moon is cold; where is the man to be found?
A blazing flame spewing out bits of coral as red as fresh blood.

討得心安臂不全
思量秪合哭蒼天
風高月冷人何處
燄發珊瑚血正鮮

Seeking in vain for his mind, he was truly at a loss;
Most bitterly he took himself and hid in the snow.
The white sweat even now is streaming down his back;
He can boast that his lungs and liver are pure and clean!

覓心無得正茫茫
最苦將身雪裏藏
脊背至今流白汗
謾言肺腑得清涼

The Fifth Patriarch Is Entrusted with the Dharma

Eminent Master Hongren, the Fifth Patriarch, in his previous lifetime was a woodcutter in the West Mountains of Qizhou. He happened to meet the Fourth Patriarch, who said to him, "I want to transmit the Dharma to you. You are already advanced in years, so if you are reborn, I will still be around." The master agreed and subsequently took birth with a woman from the Zhou family. She threw him into a dirty creek, but the gods saved and protected him.

When he was a young lad of seven, the Fourth Patriarch one day went to Huangmei county where he met the little boy, and seeing that his bones and physiognomy were unusually fine, asked him, "What is your surname?" The boy replied, "My surname is Existence-Nonexistence." The Patriarch asked, "What sort of surname (*xing*) is that?" The boy said, "It is the Buddha nature (*xing*)." The Patriarch said, "You do not have a surname then?" The boy said, "It is because my nature is empty that I have none." The Patriarch was quiet, knowing that this boy was a Dharma vessel, and took him on as an attendant. Later, after he had left the household life, the Patriarch entrusted him with the robes and the Dharma. He then went to live on the east mountain of Huangmei.[84]

五祖弘忍大師前身在蘄州西山栽松。遇四祖告曰，吾欲傳法與汝。汝已年邁，汝若再來，吾尚遲汝。師諾遂往周氏家女托生因。拋濁港中神物護持。至七歲

---

84. There are many legends and stories about Hongren, the Fifth Patriarch of Chan. This particular version can be found in a number of Song dynasty Chan sources, including the discourse records of Miaozong's contemporary, Chan Master Baiyun Shouduan 白雲守端 (1025–72). *Chan Master Baiyun Shouduan's Discourse Records* (*Baiyun Shouduan chanshi yulu*白雲守端禪師語錄) CBETA X69, 1351: 296b18–24.

為童子，四祖一日往黃梅縣，逢一小兒骨相奇秀乃問曰子何姓。曰姓即有非嘗姓。祖曰是何姓。曰是佛性。祖曰汝無姓耶。曰性空故無。祖默識是法器，即俾侍者。後令出家遂付衣法。居黃梅東山。

CHAN MASTER MIAOZONG

One goes and one comes;
One old and one young.
Two mirrors hang facing each other,
Shiny and bright, reflecting one another;
Straight and circuitous, both have been used up.
Supernatural powers and unenlightened mind:
Both of them have moved up a notch!

一去一來
一老一少
兩鏡對懸
光影俱照
直饒用盡
神通未明
向上一竅

CHAN MASTER BAOCHI

Someone grabbed and tied him up
With several rounds of rope and twine.
Straightaway he turns a somersault,
And so makes the best of a bad job.

被他捉著
重增繩索
直下翻身
將錯就錯

Chan Master Zukui

Weary, weary to the bone, he makes no effort to grasp at wisdom,
Greedy for another method to place atop another Buddhadharma.
When he comes again, he will succeed at obtaining the golden robe,
Only to find that it is the same old face as it was in the beginning!

挈挈波波不著知
貪他佛法上他機
再來圖得金襴也
可是當初舊面皮

CASE 12
The National Teacher Calls Out Three Times

One day the National Teacher called out to his attendant three times, and three times his attendant responded. The Teacher said, "I was about to say that I was being ungrateful to you, but in fact, it is you who are being ungrateful to me."[85]

國師一日喚侍者，者應諾。如是三喚三應諾。師曰，將謂吾孤負汝，卻是汝孤負吾。

CHAN MASTER MIAOZONG

Nanyang's three calls:
Waves rising without a wind.
The attendant's responses:
Like adding feet on a snake.[86]
Does the clear-eyed patch-robed monk understand or not?
Since ages past the pure breeze has been naturally vast.

南陽三喚
無風起浪
侍者應諾
為蛇安腳
明眼衲僧知不知
萬古清風自廖廓

---

85. The National Teacher referred to here is Nanyang Huizhong 南陽慧忠 (676–775).
86. In other words, unnecessary.

CHAN MASTER BAOCHI

Listen beneath the moon to the *pipa* on the river,
Its player spilling out her guts for others to hear.
At heaven's edge she bemoans the lack of a confidante,
Turning another song about the sorrows of years gone by.[87]

江上琵琶月下
聽尋嘗肝膽向
人傾天涯自惜知音
少翻作當年怨別聲

CHAN MASTER ZUKUI

Three calls and three responses:
An unbroken thread of stillness.
The clear-eyed patch-robed monk
Is left with nowhere to tap away.
Ungrateful to me, ungrateful to you—each naturally works it out;
Stop asking about Dharma ghee as opposed to poisonous herbs.[88]

三喚三諾
綿綿莫莫
明眼衲僧
無處咶啄
負吾負汝各自行
休問醍醐併毒藥

87. In the long narrative ballad entitled *Song of the Lute* (*Pipa xing* 琵琶行) by the Tang poet Bai Juyi 白居易 (772–846), the speaker tells how one night when he was enjoying himself on a river with his friends, he heard the plaintive sounds of a *pipa* being played on a boat nearby. He then discovers that the pipa-player is an aging beauty who had once been a famous courtesan in the capital, but who, with the loss of her beauty, was forced to marry a lowly merchant.

88. Ghee, or clarified butter, is regarded as being particularly rich and tasty; in Buddhism, it is used as metaphor for the highest teachings of Buddhism. Poisonous herbs, on the other hand, refers to deluded or mistaken teachings.

CASE 13
Mazu's Deafening Shouts

Chan Master Huaihai Dazhi of Mt. Baizhang in Hongzhou[89] on another occasion was attending upon Mazu. Seeing the abbot's flywhisk on the corner of his seat, Huaihai said, "Do you use that flywhisk, or do you not use it?" Mazu said, "In the future, how will you use your two flapping lips for the benefit of others?" Huaihai took the flywhisk and stood it upright. Mazu said, "Do you use that flywhisk or do you not use it?" Huaihai then took the flywhisk and hung it back up, at which Mazu let out an earth-shaking roar.

Later, some lay donors invited Huaihai to take up residence at Daxiong Mountain, the peaks of which were so steep and precipitous that it was called Baizhang.[90] One day Huaihai turned and addressed the assembly, saying, "The Buddhadharma is not a minor matter. In the past, my ears were deafened for three days by one of Mazu's shouts." When Huangbo heard this, without thinking he stuck out his tongue.

洪州百丈山懷海大智禪師，再參馬祖侍立，次祖以目視繩床角拂子。師云即此用離此用。祖曰，汝向後開兩片皮將何為人。師取拂子豎起。祖曰，即此用離此用。師以拂子掛向舊處。祖乃振威一喝。後檀信請住大雄山，峦巒峻極故號為百丈。一日顧謂眾曰，佛法不是小事。老僧昔日被馬大師一喝直得三日耳聾。黃檗聞舉，不覺吐舌。

CHAN MASTER MIAOZONG

As soon as the vital spot is struck, the poison is smeared on the drum;
The complete strategies of birthing and killing shake up past and present.

89. Huaihai Dazhi 懷海大智 (720–814), known more commonly as Baizhang Huaihai, was one of the foremost disciples of Mazu.
90. Baizhang 百丈 literally means "a hundred *zhang*." A *zhang* is a traditional Chinese unit of measurement equivalent to about ten feet.

Not till after a snow do you understand the integrity of the cypress;
Only when things get difficult, do you see the mind of a "manly man."

頂門一擊塗毒鼓
生殺全機振古今
雪後始知松柏操
事難方見丈夫心

Chan Master Baochi

A single shout was enough to make him deaf for three days;
After this all of the family traditions of Jiangxi were lost.[91]
Who'd have guessed that after hundreds of years or more,
There'd be sons and grandsons scolding the old patriarch!

一喝直教三日聾
江西從此喪家風
誰知數百餘年後
猶有兒孫罵祖翁

Chan Master Zukui

The pain is bitter when the disease fills the area below the heart;
Sons and grandsons die beneath the hooves of the immortal steed.
A single crash of thunder and a gust of pure wind rises;
Three thousand drumbeats and the coastal peaks darken.

病入膏肓苦痛深
神駒腳下喪兒孫
一聲雷振清飆起
鼓動三千海嶽昏

---

91. Jiangxi province was the area associated with Mazu and his teaching.

CASE 14
Baizhang's Fox

There was an old man who, whenever Baizhang would enter the hall, would join the assembly to listen to the Dharma. One day everybody had left except for the old man, so Baizhang asked him, "Who are you?" He said, "I am not a human being. In the past, during the time of the Kaśyapa Buddha,[92] I resided on this mountain. One day a student asked me, 'Is a person who has cultivated himself greatly still subject to cause and effect or not?' I answered, 'No, he is not subject to cause and effect.' Therefore for a hundred lifetimes I have been condemned to assume the body of a wild fox.[93] Today I ask you to say a turning phrase for me so that I may shed this wild fox's body."

Baizhang said to him, "Ask me a question." And so the old man asked him, "Is a person who has cultivated himself greatly still subject to cause and effect or not?" Baizhang replied, "He does not ignore the law of cause and effect." When the old man heard this he experienced a great enlightenment and paid reverent obeisance saying, "I have already shed my wild fox's body. I live behind the mountain; may I please ask you that you bury the monk who has just died there?" Baizhang ordered the verger to strike the gavel to announce to the congregation that after the meal, they would be holding a funeral service for a deceased monk. The assembly was startled and mystified. After the meal, Baizhang ordered the assembly to go to below the cliff behind the mountain, and with his staff he pulled out a dead fox, which he then cremated and buried according to the proper procedure.

92. The sixth of the seven ancient buddhas, immediately preceding Śākyamuni.
93. For an interesting discussion of this case, and other examples of foxlore in Chinese Chan literature, see Steven Heine, *Shifting Shape, Shaping Text: Philosophy and Folklore in the Fox Kōan* (Honolulu: University of Hawai'i Press, 1999).

That evening, Baizhang entered the hall and brought up the matter that had just transpired. Huangbo then asked, "This ancient person was mistaken concerning only a single turning phrase, and he fell into a five hundred rebirths in the body of a wild fox. If he had not made a mistake with a single turning phrase, then what would have happened?" Baizhang said, "Come closer and I will tell you." Huangbo came to the front and slapped Baizhang. Baizhang laughed and clapped his hands, saying, "It is said that barbarian's beard is red, and sure enough, here is a red-bearded barbarian!"[94]

百丈每上堂，有一老人嘗隨眾聽法。眾退唯老人不去。丈問汝何人也。曰我非人也。於過去迦葉佛時，曾住此山。因學人問大修行人還落因果也無。某甲對曰，不落。因果遂五百生墮野狐身。今請和尚代一轉語貴脫野狐身。丈曰，汝問乃問大修行人還落因果也無。丈曰不昧因果。老人言下大悟作禮曰，某甲已脫野狐身。住在山後敢乞依亡僧津送。丈令維那白椎告眾，食後送亡僧。眾驚異。食後，丈領眾至山後嵒下以杖挑出一死埜狐乃依法火葬。丈至晚上堂舉前因緣。黃蘗便問，古人錯祇對一轉語五百生墮野狐身，轉轉不錯合作箇什麼。丈曰，近前來與汝道。蘗近前與丈一掌。丈拍手笑曰，將謂胡鬚赤更有赤鬚胡。

CHAN MASTER MIAOZONG

If you aren't blind, you won't fall:
Fixing one mistake with another.
Baizhang and the dead fox
End up buried in the same hole.

不昧不落
將錯就錯
百丈埜狐
一坑埋卻

94. The red-bearded barbarian refers generally to non-Chinese Buddhist monks from India or Central Asia. Here Baizhang Huaihai would appear to be expressing his approval of Huangbo's reaction—"It seems like here is someone else who understands what is going on . . ."

CHAN MASTER BAOCHI

What is this body of a dead fox you're talking about?
His endless wild talk misleads people and alarms them.
Tut!
Now that all the interlocking roof tiles are shattered,[95]
There's no need to fight and wrangle for first place!

說甚埜狐身
無端誆惑人
咄
今朝重註破
不必競頭爭

CHAN MASTER ZUKUI

If one is not blind, one doesn't fall,
For the great void is naturally vast.
Each and every one of these manly men—
How can they be held in restraint?
When the Tai'a sword is drawn whistling from its scabbard,[96]
The black snakes slither and slink through the dense growth.

不昧與不落
太虛自寥廓
彼彼大丈夫

95. This translation is tentative, but it may possibly be an allusion to the verses from the *Dhammapada* said to be uttered by the Buddha after his enlightenment and referring to the destruction of all his delusions:
    House-builder, you are seen!
    The house you shall not build again! Broken are your rafters, all,
    Your roof beam destroyed.
John Ross Carter and Mahinda Palihawadana, trans., *Dhammapada: The Sayings of the Buddha* (Oxford and New York: Oxford University Press, 2000), 39.
96. The Tai'a was the name of a famous sword of Chinese legend that is said to have manifested its location to the poet and statesman Zhang Hua 張華 (232–300) with a purple light reaching up into the heavens.

誰能受拘縛
太阿出匣吼
青蛇左右橫斜恣盤薄.

CASE 15
Not Mind, Not Buddha

Nanquan[97] once said, "The eminent master Mazu of Jiangxi says only that 'Mind is Buddha.' But I, Old Teacher Wang, don't say that. I say 'It's not mind, it's not Buddha, it's not a thing.' Is there anything wrong in my saying this?" Zhaozhou bowed and left.

Later a monk asked Zhaozhou, "What did you, Senior Monk, mean by bowing and leaving?" Zhaozhou said, "Why don't you ask him about it?" The monk then asked Nanquan, "I've come to ask about the meaning of what the Senior Monk did." Nanquan replied, "He was able to understand my essential meaning."

南泉曰，江西馬大師秖說即心，即佛王老師不恁麼，道不是心。不是佛。不是物。恁麼道還有過麼。趙州禮拜而出。僧隨問州曰，上座禮拜了便出意作麼生，曰汝卻問取和尚。僧問泉曰，適來諗上座意作麼生。泉曰，他卻領得老僧意旨。

CHAN MASTER MIAOZONG

It is not the mind or the Buddha, it is not a thing;
Six times six is thirty-six—just as it was before.
I think of Changqing who knew to tell Inspector Lu
That he should have laughed rather then cried![98]

---

97. Nanquan Puyuan 南泉普願 (748–835), disciple of Mazu and teacher of Zhaozhou.
98. Nanquan's famous lay disciple, Inspector Lu Gen 陸亘 (765–835) who when he received news of his master's death went to the temple. Hearing the sounds of mourning, Lu burst into laughter. When asked by the head monk why he did not weep, Lu said, "If you can say something, then I will weep." Only when he realized that the monk could not answer his question, did Lu begin to cry. Later when Chan Master Changqing (Changqing Da'an 長慶大安, 793–883) heard of this, he said "The Inspector should have laughed and not cried." *Chan*

不是心佛不是物
六六依前三十六
因思長慶陸大夫
解道合笑不合哭

CHAN MASTER BAOCHI

The great strategy is perfectly clear, as the one using it knows,
But even a thread of emotion will swiftly turn into selfishness.
The determination of a "manly man" naturally soars to the heavens;
Even when seated on a needle's sharp point, he will not let it go!

Faced with a method one doesn't understand, the eyes become blind;
A powerful opponent demands that the doer know what he is doing!
Then, even if one only carries out one half of what should be done;
It won't be too late for the flash of lightning and spark of struck flint.

大用堂堂作者知
情存毫忽便成私
丈夫自有沖天志
肯坐鋒鋩未露時

當機不薦眼如癡
勍敵還須作者知
正令只堪行一半
電光石火未嫌遲

CHAN MASTER ZUKUI

Last night the wind and the thunder battled over the ford;
During the month of peach blossoms the waves are grand.

Master Foguo Yuanwu's Blue Cliff Record (*Foguo Yuanwu chanshi Biyanlu* 果圓悟禪師碧巖錄)
CBETA T 48, 2003: 153c7–11.

How many heads will sprout horns and turn into dragons,
Leaving the shrimp and crabs to glare with bulging eyes.[99]

昨夜風雷鬥孟津
桃花三級浪崢嶸
幾多頭角成龍去
蝦蟹依然努眼睛

99. Tradition has it that if a fish is able to get through the Dragon Gate (a gorge on the Yellow River located at the border of Shanxi and Shaanxi) on the third day of the third month, when the peach trees bloom, it will sprout horns and turn into a dragon. This metaphor was also used to describe students whom, having successfully passed the imperial examinations, became officials—or, in Chan texts, Chan students achieving enlightenment and becoming masters. The crabs and shrimp, by contrast, probably refer to the pedantry and inflated self-confidence of those who think they are enlightened but are very far from being so.

Case 16
Nanquan Kills the Cat

At Nanquan's monastery the east and west halls were fighting over a cat. Nanquan picked it up and said to the assembly, "Say the word and you can save the cat. If you do not say the word, then I will slice it in two." The assembly had no reply, and Nanquan then sliced the cat in two. Zhaozhou returned from outside the temple and Nanquan told him what he said. Zhaozhou then took off his grass sandals, placed them on his head, and went out. Nanquan said, "If you had been here just now, you would have been able to save the cat."[100]

南泉因東西兩堂各爭貓兒。泉遇之白眾曰,道得即救取貓兒,道不得即斬卻也。眾無對。泉便斬之。趙州自外歸泉舉前語示之。州乃脫艸履,安頭上而出。泉曰,汝適來若在,即救得貓兒也。

Chan Master Miaozong

Nanquan brandished his sword and sliced the cat in two;
Giving and taking life is something only masters understand.
The authority seems on this morning to be in his hands;
Watch carefully for when the order is to be carried out.

南泉揮劍斬貓兒
殺活唯憑作者知
權柄一朝如在手
分明看取令行時

---

100. This is one of the most famous (and unsettling!) of all Chan stories. It also appears in *The Blue Cliff Record*, cases 63 and 64.

Chan Master Baochi

Zhaozhou was secretly pleased to have claimed the advantage;
He was sure Nanquan had missed out on the first challenge.
But although he escaped with the straw sandals on his head,
Nanquan understood that there had never been a live cat!

趙州闇喜得便宜
肯信遭人第二機
頭戴草鞋雖跳出
也知不是活貓兒

Chan Master Zukui

How frightful were the talons and teeth of the wild cat;
Lifting it up, Nanquan clear-mindedly put it in the ditch.
If he'd been able to get the monks of both halls to speak,
Would Nanquan have still brought down his sword or not?

猙獰牙爪箇狸奴
提起分明付與渠
藉使兩堂俱道得
南泉還下一刀無

Below the sharp sword, both were good at turning the body;
There is nobody walking under the moon along the old road.
That which was blocked has been transmitted and flourishes;
At the golden gates, the secret armies halt by imperial decree!

狼忙刀下解翻身
古路無人帶月行
絕塞自今傳盛化
金門宣敕罷徵兵

CASE 17
Nanquan's Circle

Once Nanquan, Guizong, and Magu went together to pay a visit to National Teacher Nanyang. Along the way, Nanquan drew a circle on the ground,[101] saying, "If you all can say something, then we can go on." Guizong sat down in the middle of the circle, and Magu made a curtsey. Nanquan said, "Let's not go on then." Guizong said, "What is on your mind?" Nanquan then called out, saying, "Let's go home, let's go home."[102]

南泉與歸宗麻谷同去參禮南陽國師。 泉於路上畫一圓相道，得即去。宗便於圓相中坐谷作女人拜。泉曰，與麼則不去也。宗曰是什麼心行。泉乃相喚曰，歸去來，歸去來。

CHAN MASTER MIAOZONG

After a meal in a rustic inn, they inquire about the ford crossing;
The great masters hold their staffs protectively by their sides.
Meeting one another, words exhausted: don't go there now;
Do you think there has ever been anyone here in the forests?

埜店齋餘聊問津
作家竿木鎮隨身
相逢盡道休官去
林下何曾見一人

---

101. A teaching technique made famous by Huizhong, the "National Teacher."
102. See also *The Blue Cliff Record*, case 69. The last line of the case here in *The Blue Cliff Record* is found in the commentary rather than the main case.

Chan Master Baochi

The views of the three men were most definitely of a single kind;
How did they know the whole leopard hides in the deep hills?
Suddenly one morning the outside pillar, like life, will change,
They held on tightly to the lantern and did not let it go.[103]

總許三人見一班
那知全豹隱深山
忽朝露柱生機變
把住燈籠不放還

Chan Master Zukui

By stirring up the smoke and dust, you've already killed the principle;
How can they bear to travel for ten thousand *li*[104] for such a petty thing?
The National Teacher has never even made his residence in Nanyang;
The grass bends and the wind gusts as they pause in mid-journey.

撥動煙塵意已殊
那堪萬里共區區
國師不向南陽住
草偃風行在半途

103. The lantern here may refer to the lamp of wisdom.
104. A Chinese *li* is about a third of an English mile.

CASE 18
Layman Pang's Awakening

When Layman Pang Yun of Xiangzhou first met Shitou, he asked him, "What kind of person is not a companion of the myriad dharmas?" Shitou covered up Layman Pang's mouth with his hand, at which Pang Yun experienced sudden enlightenment. Later, Layman Pang visited Mazu and asked him, "What kind of person is not a companion of the myriad dharmas?" Mazu said, "When in a single gulp you have swallowed the entire West River, then I will tell you." Upon hearing these words, Layman Pang suddenly understood the profound principle.[105]

襄州龐蘊居士初謁石頭乃問，不與萬法為侶者是甚麼人。頭以手掩其口士，忽有省。後參馬祖問曰，不與萬法為侶者是甚麼人。祖曰，待汝一口吸盡西江水即向汝道。士於言下頓領玄旨。

CHAN MASTER MIAOZONG

With a single gulp he swallowed the West River,
Then the fine steed trampled old Pang to death.
No need to burn money and summon his ghost;
He is at peace and so is his family and country.

一口吸盡西江
馬駒踏殺老龐
不用燒錢引鬼
自然安帖家邦

---

105. Layman Pang or Pang Yun 龐蘊 (740–808) was a student of Mazu's and a famous poet. In China, he (together with his wife and daughter) is celebrated as a model of lay Buddhist practice. This incident is also referred to in Yuanwu's commentary to case 42 of *The Blue Cliff Record*.

CHAN MASTER BAOCHI

The spring colors have come to the deserted wilds;
The spring breezes blow on the willow branches.
The wooden man is able to strike the clappers;
The stone maiden knows how to play the flute.
Their marvelous tunes have neither tone nor rhyme;
Their crystalline sounds move through the vastness.
If the West River is not drunk to the last drop,
Then the ancient waves will turn rough and wild.

春色到荒郊
春風吹柳條
木人能拍板
石女解吹蕭
玅曲無音韻
清聲動沉寥
西江吸不盡
千古浪滔滔

CHAN MASTER ZUKUI

With a flick of the wrist, the arrow flies into the blue waters,
And the sleeping dragons leap up startled by this one sound.
But don't go now and spend the night by the side of the pool
Where they are exhaling ice flowers of bone-piercing cold.

劈箭飛流射碧湍
一聲驚躍睡龍蟠
如今莫向潭邊宿
吹起冰花徹骨寒

CASE 19
Daowu Sings Out Loudly

Daowu,[106] because Zhaozhou was coming, donned his tiger-skin robe and took his auspicious staff and went to the front of the main gate to wait for him. When he caught sight of Zhaozhou coming, he then sang out in a loud voice and stood up. Zhaozhou said, "Be careful of your throat." Daowu again sang out loudly and left.

道吾因趙州來，著豹皮褌，把吉撩棒在山門前等候。纔見州來，便高聲唱喏而立。州曰，小心祇候著。吾又唱喏一聲而去。

CHAN MASTER MIAOZONG

Getting an ox from someone, returning a horse—
Pacing tigers and dancing dragons: who'd dare set a price?
From three thousand li away they saw through the deception,
And gave rise to a ball of iron[107] without seam or crack.

得人一牛還人一馬
虎驟龍驤誰敢定價
三千里外見淆訛
生銹一團無縫罅

---

106. Chan Master Daowu Yuanzhi 道吾圓智 (769–835).
107. Central to the practice of huatou perfected by Dahui was cultivating a "Great Doubt," which was sometimes compared to having a ball of iron in one's throat that one could neither swallow or spit out. Ultimately, this great doubt would shatter, affording the practitioner a glimpse into true Reality.

CHAN MASTER BAOCHI

The right eye half a kilo;
The left eye eight ounces.
The stone pillar is pregnant;
The lantern claps its hands.

左眼半斤
右眼八兩
露柱懷胎
燈籠撫掌

CHAN MASTER ZUKUI

One comes out, one goes in:
As fast as wind and lightning.
The sea is drained, the mountain bare;
The ghosts wail, and the spirits weep.
The bodhisattva Guanshiyin[108]—
When will she become a buddha?

一出一入
風雷迅疾
海竭山枯
鬼號神泣
觀世音菩薩
幾時得成佛

108. Avalokiteśvara, the bodhisattva of compassion, is known in China as Guanshiyin or, alternatively, Guanyin 觀音. By the seventeenth century, this bodhisattva had come to be thought of primarily as feminine.

CASE 20
Jiashan's Awakening

When Chan Master Chuanzi Decheng[109] from Huating saw Jiashan of Shanhui coming, he said, "Your Eminence! In which temple do you reside?" Jiashan said, "I don't live in a temple and where I live is not like . . ." Chuanzi said, "Not like what?" Jiashan said, "It is not the Dharma in front of your eyes." Chuanzi said, "Where did you learn that from?" Jiashan said, "It was not somewhere that can be reached with the ears and eyes." Chuanzi said, "A single phrase and you've come up with words in the head; for ten thousand kalpas you will be like a donkey tethered to a post."

Chuanzi then said, "Although you've lowered a line a thousand feet long and are fishing in the river's depths, your hook is three inches too short; why don't you say something?" Jiashan was about to open his mouth when Chuanzi knocked him into the water with the oar. When Jiashan had clambered back on board, Chuanzi asked again, "Speak! Speak!" Jiashan was about to open his mouth, when the master hit him. Jiashan suddenly experienced a great awakening and nodded his head three times.

Chuanzi said, "The fishing rod and line are now yours; do not disturb the clear waves, and drift without intention." Jiashan then asked, "What does the teacher mean by 'cast off the fishing line and throw away the pole'?" Chuanzi said, "The fishing line hangs in the green water, and its floating and stopping is without intention." Jiashan said, "There is no path by which words can gain entry to their profound meaning; the tongue talks, but cannot say it." Chuanzi said, "When the hook has disappeared into the waves of the river, only then will the golden-scaled fish be encountered." Jiashan then covered his ears. The master said, "That's it! That's it!"

---

109. Chan Master Chuanzi Decheng 船子德诚 (820–58).

秀州華亭船子德誠禪師因夾山來參。師纔見便問，大德住甚麼寺。山曰寺即不
住，住即不似。 師曰不似是箇甚麼。山曰不是目前法。師曰，甚處學得來。
山曰，非耳目之所到。師曰一句合頭語萬劫繫驢橛。師又問垂絲千尺意在深潭
離鉤三寸子何不道。山擬開口被師一橈打落水中。山纔上船，師又曰，道道。
山擬開口，師便打山，豁然大悟乃點頭三下。師曰竿頭絲線從君弄不犯清波意
自殊。山遂問拋綸擲鉤師意如何。師曰，絲懸淥水浮定有無之意。山曰，語
帶玄而無路舌頭談而不談。師曰，釣盡江波金鱗始遇。山乃掩耳。師曰，如
是如是。

CHAN MASTER MIAOZONG

On the limitless misty waves, a leaf of a boat:
The line at the end of the pole bobs up and down.
If the hook is three inches short, what will you say?
The golden-scaled fish will secretly nod their heads.

渺渺煙波一葉舟
竿頭絲線幾沉浮
離鉤三寸如何道
便有金鱗暗點頭

CHAN MASTER BAOCHI

The line has dangled from the old cliffs for countless autumns,
And blind tortoises and lame turtles have bobbed up and down.
Suddenly they surrender to their fate, follow the hook upward;
Once the side of the boat has been crushed, stop lowering the line.

古岸垂綸不計秋
盲龜跛鱉幾沉浮
驀然負命隨鉤上
踏破船舷當下休

Only after having drifted along the rivers and lakes for several springs,
Did he meet the fisherman who pointed out the ford that he had missed.

No traces of men to be found among the peach blossoms and
jade caves;
In vain he listened among the clouds for sounds of talk and laughter.[110]

浪走江湖已數春
偶因漁父指迷津
桃花玉洞無人跡
空聽雲中笑語聲

CHAN MASTER ZUKUI

Alone he has floated his orchid boat for thirty springtimes;
The misty waves fished dry, the golden-scaled fish caught.
Then he secluded himself leaving no tracks; who knows where?
The reed flowers under the bright moon: the grief can kill you.

獨泛蘭舟三十春
煙波釣盡獲金鱗
藏身無跡知何處
明月蘆花愁殺人

110. A reference to the beloved Chinese literary myth of the Peach Blossom Spring about
a fisherman who wanders into a utopian world that, after he leaves, he is subsequently no
longer able to find.

CASE 21
The Real Buddha Sits Within

Zhaozhou entered the hall and said, "A gold buddha does not pass through the furnace; a wood buddha does not pass through the fire; a mud buddha does not pass through the water. The real buddha sits within."[111]

趙州上堂，金佛不度爐，木佛不度火，泥佛不度水，真佛內裏坐。

CHAN MASTER MIAOZONG

A gold buddha does not pass through the furnace;
The iridescent halo blazes out in the great void.
One can immediately give it one's recommendation;
There is no need to hem and to haw and to hesitate.

A wood buddha does not pass through fire;
The eyebrows of the monastery head fall out.[112]
Although the fierce flames turn the heavens red,
There is not even a fragment of relic left behind.

A mud buddha does not pass through water;
The patch-robed monk finds it hard to say a word.
As soon as he tries, he is blocked by a thousand hills
That stretch far into the distance for ten thousand li.

The real buddha sits within;
Zhaozhou stops wasting words.

111. See also *Blue Cliff Record*, case 96.
112. This refers to Zhaozhou himself; it is said that his eyebrows fell out as a result of his trying to explain the Buddhist teachings to excess.

Observing things as they are, one can deal with them,
But if you roll your eyeballs, you may miss the mark!

Gold buddha, wood buddha, mud buddha:
Once understood, they can be tossed beyond Jambudvipa.[113]
To go on and talk about the real buddha being within
Does nothing but show you're already muddleheaded.

金佛不度爐
圓光爍太虛
直下便薦得
不用更躊躇

木佛不度火
院主眉毛墮
烈燄互天紅
舍利無一顆

泥佛不度水
衲僧難下觜
擬議隔千山
迢迢十萬里

真佛內裏坐
趙州休話墮
覷體便承當
抬眸即蹉過

金佛木佛泥佛
穿來擲過閻浮
更說真佛在內
無端已被塗糊

113. In traditional Buddhist cosmology, there are four different continents; Jambudvipa is the name of the one inhabited by human beings.

Chan Master Baochi

A gold buddha does not pass through the furnace;
The colors of spring fill the imperial capital.
The hills numinous, the white clouds alive,
The earth fertile, and the yellow pulses thick.

A wood buddha does not pass through fire;
If you just let it go then you can peacefully yield.
One managed to shoot at Xuefeng's gibbon;[114]
The other completely missed Xuansha's tiger.[115]

A mud buddha does not pass through water;
Thoroughly merged, nothing left incomplete.
If you wash with water, your face will shine;
If you drink your tea, your lips will be moist.

The real buddha sits within.
By putting it into words you've made a mistake—

114. The allusion here may be to a story of Xuefeng: while walking in the forest with a fellow Chan master, he came across a band of gibbons. Seeing them, Xuefeng said, "Each of these gibbons carries an ancient mirror." His companion then asked, "The vast chiliocosm has no name—why do you single out ancient mirrors for praise?" "Now it has a scratch," Xuefeng retorted. *Eminent Teacher Xuefeng Zhenjue's Discourse Records* (*Xuefeng Zhenjue dashi yulu* 雪峰真覺大師語錄) CBETA X69, 1333: 82a17. Charles Egan notes that monkeys may suggest the "buddha mind, spontaneous and free of time and space" which is why they carry ancient mirrors. *Clouds Thick, Whereabouts Unknown: Poems by Zen Monks of China* (New York: Columbia University Press, 2010), 171.
115. In a sermon addressed to his monks, Xuansha Shibei (815–908) says, "All of you are seeing great peril. You see tigers, knives, and swords threatening your life, and you're experiencing unlimited terror. What's it like? It is like the world is painting itself with images from hell, making tigers, knives, and swords, all right there in front of you, and you feel terrified. But if you are now having such experiences then it's a terror that arises from your own personal illusions, and not something that someone else is creating for you. Do you want to understand these illusions and confused feelings? If so, then know that you have the diamond-eye. If you know this, then you realize that all the things of the world don't truly exist. So where could tigers, wolves, knives, and swords threaten you? If Shakyamuni had dealt with this like you're doing he'd never have made it." Translation by Andy Ferguson, *Zen's Chinese Heritage: The Masters and Their Teachings* (Boston: Wisdom Publications, 2000), 274.

Dug in the ground and buried yourself deeper,
So as to avoid having the true essence appear.

A gold buddha, a mud buddha, and a wood buddha;
Settling for less in front of others is ugly and foolish.
He takes the real buddha and insists on setting it apart;
Tut!
Who is this donkey tethered to the post by the gate!?

金佛不度爐
春色滿皇都
山靈白雲活
地肥黃莡粗

木佛不度火
放下便安妥
射得雪峰猴
錯過玄沙虎

泥佛不度水
圓融無不備
水洗面皮光
啜茶濕卻嘴

真佛內裏坐
出言成錯誤
掘地更深埋
免教全體露

金佛泥佛與木佛
贏得人前揚醜拙
更將真佛強分疏
咄
是甚門前繫驢橛

Chan Master Zukui

A gold buddha does not pass through the furnace,
Or else it will melt back into its original form.
Humans and gods are completely unpredictable;
Take good care of this red-whiskered barbarian!

A wood buddha does not pass through fire,
The ruddy blaze is eternally unchanging.
Resist this and your face will be charred;
Don't be surprised if there is no response!

A mud buddha does not pass through water;
The fish and dragons will rise up in formation.
If you do not know how to play with the tides,
You will be struck down into the raging waves.[116]

The real buddha sits here within;
From whence better to aim blows at the face.
If you can explain how the family is ruined,
How then could this have ever been so?

A gold buddha, a wood buddha, a mud buddha:
All on the same road but not on the same track.
If you want to know the footprints of the real buddha,
Leave and when you return tomorrow you can decide.

金佛不度爐
鎔盡舊規模
人天渾莫測
珍重赤鬚胡

---

116. The reference here is probably to the famous tidal bore of the Qiantang river near Hang-zhou, a surging spectacle that for millennia has in late summer attracted a large number of spellbound spectators.

木佛不度火
赤燄亙今古
犯著面門焦
莫怪無回互

泥佛不度水
魚龍陣方起
若非弄潮人
打入洪波裏

真佛內裏坐
好與劈面唾
自道解破家
何曾有這箇

金佛木佛泥佛
同途卻不同轍
更問真佛蹤繇
且去明朝來決

CASE 22
Zhaozhou Checks Out the Old Woman

A monk who was a disciple of Zhaozhou was traveling to Mount Wutai. He asked an old woman, "Which is the road that leads to Mount Wutai?" The old woman responded, "Just go straight ahead." After the monk had left, the old woman said, "There you have another good monk who has gone on his way." Later, when a monk asked Zhaozhou about this, Zhaozhou said, "Wait until I have checked her out."

The next day, Zhaozhou went and asked the way to Mount Wutai. The old woman said, "Just go straight ahead." After Zhaozhou had left, the old woman said, "There goes another good monk who has gone on his way." When Zhaozhou returned to the monastery he said to the monk, "I have checked out the old woman of Mount Wutai for you."

趙州因僧遊五臺問一婆子曰,臺山路向甚麼處去。婆曰驀直去。僧便去。婆曰,好箇師僧又恁麼去。後有僧舉似州,州曰,待我勘過。明日州便去問臺山路向甚處去。婆曰驀直去。州便去,婆曰好箇師僧又恁麼去。州歸院謂僧曰,臺山婆子為汝勘破了也。

CHAN MASTER MIAOZONG

Crouching at the foot of the ancient road to Tai Mountain,
Traveling monks come and go, meeting with spears and shields.
Zhaozhou lifts up the arrows of the great hero,
But once he has shot through the skeleton, he stops.[117]

117. To shoot through or "pierce the skeleton" is a Chan simile used to refer to the cutting off of all physical and mental bases of discursive thought. Someone who is free from thoughts of attachment to either samsara or nirvana is also referred to as a skeleton.

踞坐臺山古路頭
往來雲衲被戈矛
趙州提起那羅箭
穿過髑髏即便休

Chan Master Baochi

When Zhaozhou's eyeballs shoot forth a light
The old woman's brows are thrown to the ground.
Although each appears to have sealed the border,
In the end neither one is able to get themselves out.
Let's sit leisurely on top of the mountain peak
And watch as the one falls and the other rises.

趙州眼珠放光
婆子眉毛委地
雖然各占封彊
必竟不出這裏
閒來冷坐峰頭
看他一倒一起

Chan Master Zukui

Go straight ahead! Go straight ahead!
Distracted, he mistakes the road that was pointed out.
Travelling south, north, east, and west through the grasses.
How many times can he go around and back in circles?
What Zhaozhou checked out there are few who understand;
Returning home in the spring breeze, singing and dancing alone.
Tut!
That wild fox!

Pointing it out, all becomes clear, nothing to be done:
In great peace, grasses and trees exhaust the weapons of war.

The general with a single arrow penetrates the three barriers,[118]
The sun and the moon, both round, beat out a joyful melody!

驀直去驀直去
紛紛錯認指頭路
南北東西艸裏行
返擲迴旋能幾箇
趙州勘破少人知
歸對春風自歌舞
咄
這堁狐.

指出分明不奈何
太平草木盡干戈
將軍一簇三關透
日月雙圓奏凱歌

---

118. Three gates or barriers pierced by a single arrow can refer to a penetrating insight, or in this case, a single phrase or action that rids someone of all of their delusions.

CASE 23
Zhaozhou's "Go and Wash Your Bowl"

A monk asked Zhaozhou, "A student wanted to enter the monastery and begged the master for instruction." Zhaozhou asked, "Have you eaten your porridge yet?" The student answered, "Yes I have eaten my porridge." Zhaozhou said, "Then go and wash your bowl." At that the monk suddenly became enlightened.

僧問趙州，學人乍入叢林乞師指示。州曰，喫粥了也未。曰喫粥了也。州曰，洗缽盂去。其僧忽然省悟。

CHAN MASTER MIAOZONG

The ten directions pervaded by brilliance,
The eight sides lovely and most elegant.
The fine steed looks back at the shadow,[119]
The fox and hare both hide their tracks.

十方通透
八面玲瓏
駿駒顧影
狐兔潛蹤

CHAN MASTER BAOCHI

He has eaten up his porridge
And gone off to wash his bowl.

---

119. A fine horse needs only to see the shadow of the whip to take off, as opposed to a more ordinary horse who needs to feel the whip on his flesh. See note 59.

Daily necessities are ready made,
What need for anything special?

喫粥了也
洗缽盂去
日用現成
何須特地

CHAN MASTER ZUKUI

Gold is not bartered for gold,
Water is not washed by water.
The lion bites a human being;
The hound of Han chases the clod of dirt.[120]

金不博金
水不洗水
師子咬人
韓盧逐塊

---

120. A reference to the story found in the *Records of the Warring States* (*Zhanguo ce* 戰國策, compiled between the first and third centuries BCE) about a famous hound from the state of Han who was particularly good at catching rabbits. However, in the end, the fastest hound fails to catch the fastest hare, and eventually both die of exhaustion. The Chan phrase refers to a spiritual seeker who instead of chasing rabbits (essence) chases only clods of dirt (words or superficial meanings) thinking that they will bring him nourishment.

CASE 24
Does a Dog Have Buddha Nature?

A monk who was a disciple of Zhaozhou asked, "Does a dog have Buddha nature?" "No," replied Zhaozhou.

趙州因僧問，狗子還有佛性也無。州曰，無。

CHAN MASTER MIAOZONG

The iron-walled silver mountain
Was pierced by a single arrow.
That screwed-up Zhaozhou:
When he speaks, he just causes trouble.

銕壁銀山
一箭穿過
潦倒趙州
口能招禍

CHAN MASTER BAOCHI

The vastness of karmic consciousness is hard to prove;
But when Mr. Zhang drinks wine, then Mr. Li gets drunk.
Lying in the street, sleeping in the alley, blocking people's way:
Do you dare say the domestic animal is really so bad and lazy?

業識茫茫無可據
張公喫酒李公醉
倒街臥巷礙人行
敢道畜生真惡賴

CHAN MASTER ZUKUI

Zhaozhou and his dog:
If it bites you will die.
But if it possesses Buddha nature,
The poison shouldn't go that far.

趙州狗子
咬著便死
若有佛性
毒不至此

Case 25
Zhaozhou Tests Two Hermits

Zhaozhou went to where a hermit was staying and asked, "Do you have it? Do you have it?" The hermit raised a clenched fist. Zhaozhou said, "The water is shallow here—not a good place to moor a boat." He then continued traveling until he reached another hermitage, and he asked, "Do you have it? Do you have it?" The hermit also raised a clenched fist. Zhaozhou said, "You are able to let go, you are able to hold tight, you are able to kill, and you are able to bring to life." Then he bowed.

趙州到一菴主處問，有麼有麼。主豎起拳頭。州曰，水淺不是泊船處。便行又到一菴主處問，有麼有麼。主亦豎起拳頭。州曰，能縱能奪能殺能活。便作禮。

CHAN MASTER MIAOZONG

Shallow water is not the place to moor your boat;
Able to let go, able to hold tight, the proof comes naturally.
A blow of the mallet shatters the double barrier;[121]
Filling the canals, clogging the gullies: no one to face.

水淺不是泊船處
能縱能奪自有據
一椎擊碎兩重關
填溝塞壑無回互

---

121. One interpretation of this is that after passing through a barrier, one creates a second barrier by clinging to the first.

CHAN MASTER BAOCHI

Face to face, show your ability; it is time for a Dharma battle.
There are no scales light enough to measure trifling amounts.
My breast surges with hot blood; can anyone understand this?
There is only the clear breeze and the bright moon who know.

A round of three bows, but without intimacy or distance;
A foot of water can rise up in a wave of eight thousand feet.
Shatter the layered gates and walk along the living path;
Leave it to the four seas to stir up the weapons of war.

覿面呈機法戰時
無星秤子定錙銖
滿腔熱血誰能識
惟有清風明月知

聊施三拜別親疏
尺水能興萬丈波
裂破重關行活路
任教四海動干戈

CHAN MASTER ZUKUI

In both places there has been set a hidden trap for the tiger;
Between holding in and letting out, just a shade of difference.
Don't you know that the distinction lies beyond the closed fist?
Who is that heavenly steed chasing in pursuit of the wind?

兩處曾安陷虎機
收來放去絕毫釐
不知離卻拳頭外
誰是追風天馬駒

Case 26
Linji's Shout

When Linji saw a monk enter the gates, he shouted.

臨濟見僧入門便喝。

Chan Master Miaozong

Bellowing and shouting, railing away
With the energy of ten thousand men.
Discuss the Buddhadharma,
And you will still miss your move.

喑嗚叱吒
萬人氣索
佛法商量
猶欠一著

Chan Master Baochi

Unsheath the Blown-Hair Sword to deal with the uneven;[122]
Its glowing divine light shines and encompasses all.
Piercing through the skeleton, startling heaven and earth;
Who'd believe there was no such man in the Great Tang!

出匣吹毛為不平
神光閃爍自消魂

---

122. The sharpness of a sword is tested by blowing a hair against its blade: if the hair splits of itself, then the sword can be considered to be sharp indeed. Here the sword symbolizes wisdom that cuts off attachment.

髑髏穿過驚天地
誰信大唐無個人

CHAN MASTER ZUKUI

This single shout of Linji's—
What a piece of shit it is!
Countless green maggots
Have yet to gnaw it through.

臨濟一喝
是什屎橛
無限青蠅
咀嚼不徹

CASE 27
The True Man Without Rank

Linji instructed the assembly, saying, "In all of you lumps of red flesh, there is a true man without rank who is always going in and out of the gates of your face. Those of you have not yet had evidence of this, then look, look!" At that time there was a monk who came forward and asked, "What is a true man without rank like?" Linji came down from his meditation cot and grabbed him, saying, "Speak! Speak!" The monk was about to explain, when Linji let go of him, saying, "What a piece of shit is this true man without rank!"

臨濟示眾曰，汝等諸人赤肉團上，有一無位真人嘗向諸人面門出入。未證據者看看。時有僧出問，如何是無位真人。濟下禪床擒住云，道道。僧擬議。濟拓開云，無位真人是什麼乾矢橛。

CHAN MASTER MIAOZONG

Casting the imprint, melting the seal:
Completely raising the true command.
To know the principle of the lineage,
Do not deviate by a blink of the eye.

鑄印銷印
全提正令
要識綱宗
不隔一瞬

CHAN MASTER BAOCHI

The true man without rank has come and gone;
The bed-wetting devil keeps stinking things up.
Stop garlanding this ape with fragrant grasses;
In a wink, flowers fade in the spring wind.

The true man without rank has donkey feet and Buddha hands,
Wandering around hills and streams, tipping over the universe.
Look up at him in front of you, then suddenly he is behind you;
In a wink, his eyebrows will all start to fall out, will all fall out.

無位真人嘗出入
尿床鬼子無巴鼻
休將芳草殢王孫
春風眨眼花狼藉

無位真人驢腳佛手
旋轉河山掀翻宇宙
瞻之在前忽焉在後
眨上眉毛漏逗漏逗

CHAN MASTER ZUKUI

Below the gate of Mount Jing, things seem fine,[123]
But within the hall of Linji, there is a big mistake.
If you want to understand the true man without rank,
You shouldn't lean on the gate or stand by the door.

徑山門下彷彿
臨濟堂中太錯
要識無位真人
不得倚門傍戶

123. Dahui Zonggao, Miaozong's teacher, lived for a long time on Mount Jing, in Zhejiang province.

CASE 28
Linji's Host and Guest

When Linji ascended the dais, the head monks from the two halls looked at each other and simultaneously let out a shout. A monk asked the master, "Was there a guest and a host or not?" The master said, "The guest and the host were obvious."

The master instructed the assembly, saying, "If you want to understand Linji's phrase about the guest and the host, go and ask the two head monks of the hall."

臨濟上堂次兩堂首座相見同時下喝。僧問師還有賓主也無。師曰賓主歷然。師召眾曰，要會臨濟賓主句，問取堂中二首座。

CHAN MASTER MIAOZONG

One shout confronts the student as guest and host are distinguished;
Don't use conceptual understanding to emphasize intimate and far.
Flipping over his body, the lion is so magnificent and fierce;
If the eyes are not sharply sighted, the whole world is a guest.

一喝當機賓主分
莫將知見強疏親
反身師子威獰甚
眼裏無筋一世貧

CHAN MASTER BAOCHI

Two mouths share a single tongue;[124]
Rain disperses, the universe is vast.

124. See Zhang Dayuan's preface.

The sword has severed the snakes and dragons,
But the turtle in the clay jar has got away.

兩口同一舌
雨散長空闊
仗劍斬龍蛇
甕中走卻鱉

CHAN MASTER ZUKUI

Through the flash of lightning comes the crash of thunder;
Claws and teeth have not yet exposed the complete method.
The blind tortoise and lame turtle no longer feel surprised;
When you've trapped the divine dragon you can ride it home.

閃電光中霹靂飛
爪牙猶未露全機
盲龜跛鱉休驚怪
擒得神龍便跨歸

CASE 29
Xuefeng's Gobblers of Dregs

Xuefeng knocked on Wushi's[125] door. "Who is it?" Wushi inquired. "The son of the male and female phoenix," replied Xuefeng. "What are you up to?" asked Wushi. "I have come to chew on Old Guan." Wushi opened the door and grabbing hold of Xuefeng said, "Speak! Speak!" When Xuefeng hesitated, Wushi kicked him out and closed the door. Afterward, Xuefeng instructed the assembly, saying, "At that time if I had been able to enter the gate of Old Guan, what would you bunch of gobblers of dregs have to grope for?"

烏石因雪峰扣門，石問，誰。峰云，鳳凰兒。石曰，作麼生。峰曰，來啗老觀。石開門搊住曰，道道。峰擬議，石便托開掩卻門。峰住後示眾云，我當時若入得老觀門，你這一隊噇酒糟漢，向甚處摸索.

CHAN MASTER MIAOZONG

The full-grown son of the feathered and winged phoenix,
Happened to get it all wrong there below Old Guan's gate.
In the still silence, he suddenly remembered an old debt,
And returning to say goodbye, tried to gain the advantage.[126]

養成羽翼鳳凰兒
老觀門下偶差池
冷地忽然思舊債
卻來別處討便宜

---

125. Chan Master Wushi Lingguan 烏石靈觀, referred to here as "Old Guan," was a disciple of Huangbo Xiyun 黃檗希運 (751–850).
126. Literally, "takes advantage"—in other words, he seeks to achieve great results through an easy trick or method.

Chan Master Baochi

"Thinking I was Hou the White,
He turned out to be Hou the Black."[127]
Bobbing up and down, suddenly they meet;
What is inauspicious before won't be lucky later.
You may spare him and let him to come in the door,
But you will not avoid personally meeting the thief![128]

我早猴白
伊更猴黑
沒興忽相逢
前凶後不吉
饒伊入得門
未免親遭賊

Chan Master Zukui

The phoenix is not just an ordinary bird;
How would he willingly be held captive in a cage?

127. This line refers to a story recorded by the Song dynasty writer Qin Guan 秦观 (1049–ca. 1100) in his "The Story of the Two Hou's." In Fujian lived a certain Hou the White who was known for his wit and prescience: no one dared to challenge him. One day, he met a woman named Hou the Black on the road standing at the side of a well, leaning over it as if she had lost something. Curious, Hou the White asked her about it. Hou the Black said, "Unfortunately, I lost my earring in the well—it is worth a hundred gold coins! I will reward the person who can retrieve it with one half of that sum. Would you be interested?" Hou the White thought about it for a while: "This woman has lost her earring. If I am able to get it, I can keep it and not return it." And so he agreed, and taking off his clothes, he slowly descended the well. When he had got down to the water, Hou the Black took all of his clothes and ran away and was never found again. Ever since then, when the people of Fujian engage in commerce, they say, "I am already Hou the White, then you are Hou the Black." The meaning is "I came thinking to cheat you, but I was ripped off myself instead." In the kōan, Xuefeng is saying, "I thought I would be the one to see through him; who would have guessed that I would be the one to be seen through by him!" Or, "I thought I was the one with the insight, who would have known that his insight was even greater than mine!"
128. The thief here refers to describe the work of a Chan master or the effectiveness of a Chan kōan—in other words, you can try to get in the door another way, but in the end you will have to come face to face with the challenge presented by the master.

He flew up toward the nine heavens but didn't stay there,
Because that Old Guan has gone and kicked over his nest.

In the family customs of the ancients there are no spots or flaws,
So open up that stone man and check out the snakes and dragons.
Xuefeng did not even manage to get inside the gate;
He spent his time wandering aimlessly on the road.

鳳凰不是凡間鳥
爭肯將身入網羅
飛向九霄猶未住
賺他老觀踏翻窠

古老家風絕點瑕
打開石人驗龍蛇
雪峰不得其門入
往往途中亂撒沙

CASE 30
Deshan's Blows

Whenever Deshan saw a monk enter the gate he would hit him.[129]

舉德山凡見僧入門便棒。

CHAN MASTER MIAOZONG

Killing and bringing to life simultaneously:
The poison and the Dharma nectar together.
Is it a punishment? Is it reward?
Your guess is as good as mine!

殺活並行
醍醐毒藥
是賞是罰
一任卜度

CHAN MASTER BAOCHI

A single white-colored staff
Thrusts up to the great Heaven.
When it comes, it cuts off a thousand roads,
Startling the turtle-nosed snake of South Mountain,[130]
Without moving, catching buddhas and patriarchs.

129. Just as Linji was famous for his shouts, Chan master Deshan Xuanjian 德山宣鑑 (782–865) was famous for his blows.
130. Case 22 of *The Blue Cliff Record* is entitled "Xuefeng's Turtle-Nosed Snake." The commentary to this case says, "This turtle-nosed snake is unavoidably hard to handle; you must know how to handle it before you can do so. Conversely, if you don't know how to handle it,

一條白棒掀天大
都來劃斷千差路
驚起南山鱉鼻蛇
不動纖毫擒佛祖

Chan Master Zukui

With a single blow of Deshan's,
The Buddhadharma was exhausted.
What then about things nowadays?
The Old Barbarian must be in despair!

德山一棒
佛法盡喪
總似今日
老胡絕望

---

you'll be bitten by the snake." In the same commentary it says, "Suddenly [Xuefeng] thrusts out his staff. From the beginning the snake has been right here. You must not then go to the staff for sustenance. Yunmen took his staff and threw it down in front of [Xuefeng], making a gesture of fright. Thus [Yunmen] used his staff as the turtle-nosed snake." See Cleary and Cleary, 151–52. See also case 34 of this volume.

CASE 31
Xinghua Levies a Penalty

Xinghua[131] addressed duty-distributor[132] Kebin, saying, "In a short while you will be the teacher in charge." Kebin said, "I will not enter into this company." The master said, "Do you not enter having understood, or do you not enter not having understood?" Kebin said, "I won't say." The master then struck him, saying, "Duty-distributor Kebin has lost this Dharma battle; the penalty is five strings of cash with which to prepare a special meal for the entire assembly." The next day, the master himself took the gavel and announced that since Kebin the duty-distributor had not won the Dharma battle, he was not allowed to eat. Kebin then left the monastery.

興化謂克賓維那日，汝不久為唱導之師。賓曰，不入這保社。師曰，會了不入，不會了不入。曰總不與麼。師便打曰，克賓維那法戰不勝罰錢五貫，設饌飯一堂。次日，師自白槌克賓維那法戰不勝，不得喫飯。即便出院。

CHAN MASTER MIAOZONG

Xinghua struck Kebin:
With each blow a scar.
Although the ancient ones have already gone,
They have left us with an exemplary model.
Thirty years from now,
Who will appreciate this kindness?

興化打克賓
一棒一條痕

---

131. Chan master Xinghua Cunjiang 興化存獎 (830–88) was one of Linji's few Dharma successors.
132. The monk responsible for supervising the work and job assignments at the monastery.

古人雖已往
留得典刑存
三十年後
幾箇知恩

CHAN MASTER BAOCHI

When Xinghua's wind blows, the grasses bend;
Kebin lost his money and received a scolding.
Turning the method-wheel to enlightenment,
Flint spark and lightning glow are hard to distinguish.
Double radiance, double darkness completely gathered in:
Whether sage or commoner, both will be left behind.
An entire day of wind and rain has fixed everything up:
Red smartweed and white duckweed on both riverbanks.

興化風行艸偃
克賓失錢遭譴
打翻向上機輪
石火電光難辨
雙明雙暗全收
是聖是凡齊遣
一天風雨脩然
紅蔘白蘋兩岸

CHAN MASTER ZUKUI

In front of Xinghua's hall, the Dharma battle is a new one,
As everything in the whole world returns to humaneness.
Crimson banners glorious in the face of the clear breeze—
If he is in the right, make him reach out somewhere else.

興化堂前法戰新
普天率土盡歸仁
赤幡卓出清風面
有理教渠別處伸

CASE 32
Chen Cao Checks Out the Monks

The censor of Muzhou, Grand Secretary Chen Cao, was visiting Muzhou Daozong.[133] One day he climbed a tower with a group of his officials. They caught sight of several monks traveling toward them. One of the officials said, "Those who are coming are all wandering monks." Chen said, "No they aren't." The man said, "How do you know that they are not?" Chen said, "Wait until they come closer and then I will check them out for you." After a little while, the monks arrived at the foot of the tower and Chen suddenly called out "Oh honorable monks!" The monks all raised their heads. Chen then said to all of the officials, "And you didn't believe what I told you!"[134]

睦州刺史陳操尚書見睦州。一日與僚屬登樓，次見數僧行來。一官人曰，來者總是行腳僧。公曰不是。曰焉知不是。公曰待來勘過。須臾僧至樓前，公驀喚，上座。僧皆舉首。公謂諸官曰，不信道。

CHAN MASTER MIAOZONG

Grab the drum, grasp the banners, test the patchrobed monks,
Then exchange two black beans for the two pupils of the eyes.
Over the years, he has withered away from the snow and frost,
And so he is startled by the sight of the falling willow catkins.

奪鼓攙旗驗衲僧
便將黑豆換雙睛
昔年曾被雪霜苦

---

133. Chen Cao was a government official and lay disciple of Tang dynasty Chan master Muzhou Daozong (780–877)
134. See also *The Blue Cliff Record*, case 33.

看見楊花落也驚

CHAN MASTER BAOCHI

One going east, one going west: the streams inside the dikes;
One gathering, one scattering: the clouds at heaven's edge.
One coming and one going: the travelers along the road;
One topsy and one turvy: the threads of hemp in the pond.

一東一西隴頭水
一聚一散天邊霞
一來一往道上客
一顛一倒池中麻

CHAN MASTER ZUKUI

The arrow or the blade: if there is a road one must check it out.
Medicine or taboo: he is skilled at the arts of transformation.[135]
If one is called one must turn one's head—no time for thinking;
It is but a response to a mournful wind that has stirred for ages.

箭鋒有路看謀略
藥忌知誰善變通
喚得回頭無勘處
祇應千古動悲風

135. The translation of this line is tentative.

CASE 33
Yantou the Ferryman

When Yantou was in Shatai, he was a ferryman on a lake in Ezhou. On each side of the lake hung a board; when someone wanted to cross he or she would knock on the board. Yantou would call out, "Who is it?" or "Which side are you crossing to?" Then he would wave his oars, come out from the reeds, and go to meet the traveler. One day a woman carrying a child in her arms appeared and said, "I have nothing to ask you about plying the oar or handling the pole," she said, "But where did the child I am holding in my arms come from?" He struck the woman with the oar. The woman said, "I have given birth to seven children; six of them didn't meet anyone who truly understood them, and this one will not be any good either." She then threw it into the water.

嵒頭值沙汰於鄂渚湖邊作渡子。兩岸各掛一板，有人過渡打板一下，頭曰阿誰。或曰要過那邊去，頭乃舞棹迎之。一日因一婆抱一孩兒來乃曰，呈橈舞棹即不問，且道婆手中兒甚處得來。頭便打。婆曰，婆生七子六箇不知音，秖這一箇也不消得。便拋向水中。

CHAN MASTER MIAOZONG

A leaf of a boat drifts across the vast stretch of water;
Lifting and dancing his oars, he sings to a different tune.
Mountain clouds and ocean moon: both are tossed away;
The battle won, Zhuang Zhou's butterfly dream carries on.

一葉扁舟泛渺茫
呈橈舞棹別宮商
山雲海月多拋卻
贏得莊周蝶夢長

CHAN MASTER BAOCHI

This sudden encounter and the order is carried out:
In the excess space, a piece of an old woman's mind.[136]
In this case, if she flings the child into the billowing waves,
I doubt it will kill the eloquent and glib people of this world.

驀劄相逢正令行
空餘一片老婆心
而今抛入洪波裡
疑殺滔滔天下人

CHAN MASTER ZUKUI

Opening up the river flow, traces of moon appear;
The dirt and dust of the world sink into the cold.
Dreams return to the song sung by the fisherman;
Twisting and turning, settling the Buddha-mind is hard!

劃破江流露月痕
塵沙剎土冷沉沉
夢回一棹漁歌裏
曲曲難安佛祖心

136. Also translatable as "grandmotherly heart," a term often used to refer to the tough but compassionate love exercised by Chan masters toward their disciples.

CASE 34
Xuefeng's Turtle-Nosed Snake

Xuefeng entered the hall and said, "In South Mountain there is a turtle-nosed snake.[137] All of you should really go have a good look." Changqing went out and said, "Today in the hall there was one person who lost both his body and his life." Yunmen took his staff and flung it in front of Xuefeng, with a gesture as of fright.

There was a monk who raised this with Xuansha[138] who said, "It may be that elder brother Leng [Changqing] is like this, but I am not." The monk asked, "What do you say, Master?" Xuansha said, "Why make use of 'South Mountain?'"[139]

雪峰上堂，南山有一條鱉鼻蛇。汝等諸人切須好看。長慶出曰，今日堂中大有人喪身失命。雲門以拄杖攛向峰前，作怕勢。有僧舉似玄沙。沙曰，須是稜兄始得然，雖如是，我即不然。和尚曰，作麼生。沙曰，用南山作麼。

CHAN MASTER MIAOZONG

The old man of Xianggu Mountain[140] was instructing his followers;
When he paused to deliberate, he received a mouthful from another.
The glory of springtime suddenly burst out and startled everyone,
But unable to avoid the tip of his own sword, he wounded his hand.

---

137. This snake is a metaphor for the Great Death. All those wishing to attain enlightenment must be swallowed by this snake—and come out the other end.
138. Xuansha Shibei (835–908).
139. See also *The Blue Cliff Record*, case 22.
140. In 865, Xuefeng Yicun (822–908), moved to Xianggu Mountain in Fuzhou (located in present day Fujian province), where he established one of the most flourishing monastic centers of the time.

象骨老人示徒
擬議遭他一口
韶陽突出驚人
未免傷鋒犯手

CHAN MASTER BAOCHI

The turtle-nosed snake of South Mountain is extraordinarily strange;
There is no way it can be drawn and there is no way it can be painted.
If you play with it, its rancid-smelling fumes will fill the great Tang;[141]
Dare I inquire what patch-robed monk has ever even seen its bones?

南山鱉鼻多奇特
描不成兮畫不得
播弄腥風滿大唐
敢問衲僧誰見骨

CHAN MASTER ZUKUI

Summoning is easy, chasing away is hard,
If in losing the body and self one vacillates.
The staff tip suddenly thrust out startles everyone.
Hold on to South Mountain and look at it carefully:
Mist vague and hazy, grasses overgrown and wild.
Although Old Xue pretends to be an old hand,
When you think about it, what he says is nonsense.

呼即易遣即難喪
身失命太顛頂
杖頭突出驚人
膽拈卻南山仔細看
煙冉冉草漫漫雪老
雖然好手箏
來也是無端

141. The Great Tang refers to the entirety of China.

CASE 35
Xuefeng's Twenty Blows

Xuefeng asked a monk, "Where have you come from?" The monk said, "From Fuchuan's place."[142] Xuefeng said, "You have yet to cross the sea of life and death, so why have you gone and overturned the boat?" The monk could not say anything. He then returned to Fuchuan and told him about this. Fuchuan said, "Why didn't you say 'It does not depend on life and death.'" The monk again went to Xuefeng and presented him with these words. Xuefeng said, "These are not your words." The monk said, "No, they are Fuchuan's words." Xuefeng said, "I have twenty blows to send to Fuchuan and twenty blows that I myself must suffer as well for interfering in your affairs."

雪峰問僧，近離甚處。曰覆船。峰曰，生死海未渡，為甚麼覆卻船。僧無語。乃回舉似覆船。船曰何不道，渠無生死。僧再至雪峰進此語。峰曰，此不是汝語。曰是覆船恁麼道。峰曰，我有二十棒寄與覆船，二十棒老僧自喫，不干闍黎事。

CHAN MASTER MIAOZONG

Still lost in the sea of birth and death, he's not yet crossed over:
Transmitting words, passing on phrases, how many thousands!
With just a single blow, the sea-carp is flipped over:
The one who was lost immediately becomes crazy wise.

生死海中猶未渡
傳言送語幾千程
一棒打翻東海鯉
迷人直下便狂惺

---

142. Chan Master Fuchuan Hongjian 覆船洪荐. "Fuchuan " also means "overturned boat."

CHAN MASTER BAOCHI

The sea of life and death has not yet been crossed,
But a single word can already provide instructions.
He is mature and so the returning spirit is fragrant,
While I grab the drum that is smeared with poison
And at the same time grasp the tiger's head and tail—
The sweet one is sweet and the bitter one is bitter.

生死海未渡
一語先分付
渠熱返魂香
伊擖塗毒鼓
虎頭虎尾一時收
甜者甜兮苦者苦

CHAN MASTER ZUKUI

The sea of life and death has not yet been crossed;
How then can he have overturned the boat?
Damming the flow, he puts forward a question
That should cause the ocean to immediately dry up.
Twenty black wisteria vines in the bitter cold wind:
Don't make those with a mouth pass on borrowed words.

生死海未渡
如何覆卻船
截流伸一問
滄溟立須乾
二十烏藤風凜凜
莫教有口借人傳

CASE 36
Lan'an's Being and Nonbeing

Chan Master Shushan Guangren of Fuzhou[143] heard that the monk Guishan Lan'an from Fuzhou instructed the assembly, saying, "'Being' and 'nonbeing' are like wisteria vines clinging to a tree." The master went into the mountains to look for Lan'an and found him plastering a wall. He asked him, "I have heard you say that 'being' and 'nonbeing' are like wisteria vines clinging to a tree. Is this so?" Lan'an said, "Yes, it is so." The master asked, "If suddenly the tree topples over and the wisteria vines wither, then where will 'being' and 'nonbeing' go to?" Lan'an put down his pan of mud and, laughing, returned to the abbot's quarters. The Master said, "I have come three thousand *li* and sold my clothes just to see you about this matter. How can you play around with me like this?" Lan'an said to his attendant, "Bring two hundred silver coins and give it to this monk." Lan'an then said to Shushan, "Later there will be a one-eyed dragon whose pointers will help you break though."

Later Shushan heard about the monk Mingzhao Deqian from Wuzhou, and so he went to pay him his respects.[144] Mingzhao asked him, "Where have you come from?" The Master said, "I have come from Minzhong" [Fujian province]. Mingzhao said, "Did you go to Lan'an's?" The Master said, "I did." Mingzhao said, "When you went to see him, what did he say?" The Master told him what he had said. Mingzhao said, "Lan'an can

---

143. Chan Master Shushan Guangren 疏山匡仁 (837–909) was a disciple and Dharma heir of Dongshan Liangjie (807–69), although he also studied under a number of other teachers including one by the name of Changqing Da'an 長慶大安 (793–883), also known as Lan'an 嬾安. He is also sometimes referred to as Guishan Lan'an 潙山嬾安 because he came from Mt. Gui (Guishan) in Hunan province. In the Chinese original text, he is referred to as Dagui 大潙 or Great Gui.

144. The tenth-century Chan master Mingzhao Deqian 明招德謙 was known for his skills in Dharma combat and taught in Wuzhou 婺州 (today the city of Jinhua 金華 in Zhejiang province) for forty years. He is also said to have been blind in one eye.

be said to be correct at the head and correct at the tail; it is just that he has not yet met up with someone who understands him." The Master still did not understand and again asked what would happen to the words if the tree toppled and the wisteria vines withered. Mingzhao said, "You will have made Lan'an laugh again!" When the Master heard these words, he was greatly enlightened. And so he said, "From the beginning there was a knife hidden in Lan'an's laughter." He then bowed deeply and acknowledged his error.

撫州疏山光仁禪師聞福州大溈安和尚示眾曰，有句無句，如藤倚樹。師特入嶺，到彼值溈泥壁，便問，承聞和尚道有句無句，如藤倚樹，是否。曰是。師曰，忽然樹倒藤枯句歸何處。溈放下泥盤，呵呵大笑，歸方丈。師曰，某甲三千里賣卻布單特為此事而來，何得相弄。溈喚侍者取二百錢與這上座去，遂囑曰，向後有獨眼龍為子點破。在後聞婺州明招謙和尚出世，徑往禮拜。招問甚處來。師曰閩中來。招曰，曾到大溈否。師曰到。曰有何言句。師舉前話，招曰，溈山可謂頭正尾正，秪是不遇知音。師亦不省，復問樹倒藤枯句歸何處。招曰，卻使溈山笑轉新。師於言下大悟，乃曰溈山元來笑裡有刀，遙禮悔過。

CHAN MASTER MIAOZONG

Being and nonbeing
Like vines clinging to a tree.
Xuansha cracks the board;
Heshan beats the drum.[145]
Don't you know, sir, the saying of Xuedou?[146]
"If you want to be a teacher of gods and men,
That which stands before you is the tiger itself!"[147]

---

145. See *The Blue Cliff Record*, case 44. The phrase refers to Heshan's reply to questions put to him by a monk, including "What is the real truth?" Answer: "Knowing how to beat the drum."

146. Xuedou Chongxian (980–1052).

147. In the discourse records of Xuansha Shibei (815–908) we read how one day he went into the mountains with a fellow Chan master. When his friend pointed out the fact that there was a tiger ahead, Xuansha brought up a comment attributed to Xuedou Zhongxian: "If you take both men and gods to be your teacher, then before you everything will be a tiger." See *Xuansha Shibei chanshi yulu*, 361.

有句無句如藤倚樹
玄沙斫牌禾山打鼓
君不見雪寶有語兮
要與人天為師
面前端的是虎

CHAN MASTER BAOCHI

When he sold off all his clothes, he stirred up trouble:
Ten thousand miles a trifle as the road twisted and turned.
In his laugh there was a knife that could inflict a wound;
To this very day the world is full of such lies and deceits!

布單賣卻起奔波
萬里區區路轉多
笑裏有刀傷痛處
至今天下有淆訛

CHAN MASTER ZUKUI

Tiger's head and tiger's tail simultaneously gathered in;
The laughter stops as a fierce wind circles the Nine Provinces.[148]
On this day the weapons of war have all been silenced;
I don't know where one can go in search of a noble title.

虎頭虎尾一時收
笑罷雄風遍九州
此日干戈齊偃息
不知何處覓封侯

148. Jiuzhou 九州 ("The Nine Provinces") is an ancient term for China.

CASE 37
Bajiao's Staff

Chan Master Bajiao Huiqing[149] of Zhengzhou entered the hall and holding up his staff said, "If you have a staff, I'll give you a staff. If you don't have a staff, I'll take the staff away from you." Then, leaning on his staff, he descended from his seat.

郢州芭蕉山慧清禪師上堂，拈拄杖曰，你有拄杖子我與你拄子，你無拄杖子我奪卻你拄杖子。靠拄杖子下座。

CHAN MASTER MIAOZONG

When Bajiao raised up his staff,
Everything in the cosmos was startled!
Frogs may have leapt all the way to India,
But his eyebrows still rest above his eyes.

芭蕉舉起拄杖
驚動森羅萬象
蝦蟆飛過梵天
眉毛元在眼上

CHAN MASTER BAOCHI

When Bajiao lifted up his staff,
Everything in the world lost its nerve!

---

149. The tenth-century monk Bajiao Huiqing 芭蕉慧清 was a Korean Chan master who came to China to study and eventually settled on Mount Bajiao in Hubei province, from which he took his name.

If I had grabbed it and snapped it in half,
What then would he have had to lean on?

芭蕉舉起拄杖
萬象森羅膽喪
我若奪來拗折
看你有甚倚傍

CHAN MASTER ZUKUI

When Bajiao lifted up his staff,
He exposed his innards and entrails.
If the patch-robed monks had all realized it then,
They'd have avoided having it land on their heads.

芭蕉舉起拄杖
露出心肝五臟
衲僧自合知時
免教落在頭上

CASE 38
Baofu's Unpolished Mind

When Baofu's[150] attendant stood up, Baofu asked him, "What is this unpolished mind that you've attained?" The attendant said, "Where is this so-called unpolished mind of mine?" Baofu then picked up a clod of dirt and handing it to the monk said, "Toss this out in front of the gate." When the monk had tossed it out, he came back and then asked, "Where is this so-called unpolished mind?" Baofu said, "It was because I saw a builder and a stonemason that I said that you had an unpolished mind."

保福因僧侍立問曰，汝得恁麼麤心。曰甚麼處是某甲麤心處。福拈一塊土度與僧曰，拋向門前著。僧拋了卻來曰，甚處是某甲麤心處。福曰我見築著磕著，所以道汝麤心。

CHAN MASTER MIAOZONG

At dawn and at noon, rice-gruel vegetarian meals:
Lay out the bowls, unroll the mat, and when you're full take a nap.
If both the builder and the stonemason are recommended,
Then even when things are not in fashion, they'll be in style.

晨朝有粥齋時飯
展缽開單飽便休
築著磕著如薦得
不風流處也風流

Chan Master Baochi

When summoned, you come; when dispatched, you leave,
But it is hard to avoid having to touch the stonemason.
Suddenly, the one who steps into it laughs, "Ha! Ha!"
The grass sandals on his feet are actually his own!

喚汝即來遣即去
觸著磕著難迴避
驀然踏著笑呵呵
腳下草鞋自家底

Chan Master Zukui

The patch-robed monk unwittingly touches the stonemason;
One step forward and he shakes up Heaven and stirs up Earth;
One step backward and he fills the canals and clogs the gullies.
Whimpering, he thinks about melting stone to patch up Heaven;
Why does it seem so misty and nebulous as if not yet chiseled?

觸著磕著衲僧罔覺
進一步兮搖乾蕩坤
退一步兮填溝塞壑
噁因思煉石補天
何似鴻濛未鑿

CASE 39
Every Day Is a Good Day

Yunmen instructed his assembly, saying, "I am not asking you about it before the fifteenth day; but see if you can come up with something about it after the fifteenth day." When the assembly did not respond, he himself answered for them: "Every day is a good day."

雲門示眾曰，十五日已前不問汝，十五日已後道將一句來。眾無對。自代曰，日日是好日。

CHAN MASTER MIAOZONG

Every day is a good day:
The Buddha's law and the world's law both complete.
There is no need to specially seek out the secret and mysterious;
All you need to worry about is that both basin and bowl are wet.

日日是好日
佛法世法盡周畢
不須特地覓幽玄
只管缽盂兩度濕

CHAN MASTER BAOCHI

On clear days, the sun comes out;
When it rains, the earth is damp.
There is no need to think about anything else,
Except being able to finish up your business.

天晴日頭出
雨落地下濕
不用別思量
管教能事畢

Chan Master Zukui

The level can't be maintained, the danger can't be extracted:
Whether in Heaven above or the human world, how many?
Shattering the pearl of the beautiful bright moon,
Knocking the five-colored bones of the phoenix.
Stop! Stop!
Sir, don't you see that there are words on this stone?
Having received these words you must know the teachings,
So don't try to establish your own rules and regulations!

平不留險非取
天上人間能幾幾
撲碎驪龍明月珠
敲出鳳凰五色髓
止止
君不見石頭有語兮
承言須會宗
勿自立規矩.

Case 40
Chen Cao Asks about the Teachings

When Yunmen went to Jianzhou, Grand Secretary Chen Cao invited him to a vegetarian meal. When they met, Chen asked him, "As for what's in the Confucian texts, I won't ask you about that; and as for the general meaning of the twelve divisions and the three vehicles,[151] you are an expert in that. So what is the reason for this journey on foot that you have undertaken?" Yunmen said, "How many people have you asked this question?" Chen Cao said, "Today I am only asking you." Yunmen said, "Putting aside today's question for a moment, let me ask you: what is the meaning of the teachings?" Chen Cao replied, "Yellow scrolls on red rollers." Yunmen said, "Those are just words and letters, what do those have to do with the meaning of the teaching?" Chen Cao said, "The mouth wants to speak of it, but the words disappear; the mind seeks an affinity with it, but the thoughts vanish." Yunmen said, "'The mouth wants to speak of it, but the words disappear' refers to verbalization; 'The mind seeks an affinity with it, but the thoughts vanish,' refers to false thinking. What is the general meaning of the teachings?" Chen Cao was at a loss for words.

Yunmen asked, "I have heard it said that the Grand Secretary has read the *Lotus Sūtra*: is that right?" Chen Cao said, "That is right." Yunmen said, "In this sūtra it says that 'making a living and conducting business is not mutually opposed to the material reality.' But it is also said that in the realm beyond thinking and non-thinking, a number of people have

---

151. The three vehicles are the śrāvaka vehicle (through which one reaches realization through the teachings of Buddha), the pratekya vehicle (realization through self-awakening), and the bodhisattva vehicle (realization through understanding of the highest level of *bodhi* or wisdom). The twelve divisions is a traditional classification of the Buddhist teachings. The "three vehicles and twelve divisions" refer to the Buddhist teachings, especially those contained in the written texts. Chan rhetoric often speaks of not relying on such texts, but rather seeking an unmediated experience of reality.

backed away from this stand."[152] The Grand Secretary was at a loss for words.

Yunmen said, "The Grand Secretary must not be too careless. Even monks who discarded the three scriptures and five commentaries and entered the monastery ten or twenty years ago still find themselves at a loss. How can you expected to be able to be able to answer?" The Grand Secretary bowed and said, "I have erred."[153]

雲門到江州，陳操尚書請齋，纔見便問，儒書中即不問，三乘十二分教自有座主。作麼生是衲僧行腳事。門曰，曾問幾人來。曰，即今問上座。門曰，即今且置，作麼生是教意。曰，黃卷赤軸。門曰，這箇是文字語言，作麼生是教意。曰，口欲談而辭喪，心欲緣而慮忘。門曰，口欲談而辭喪，為對有言。心欲緣而慮忘為對妄想。作麼生是教意。書無語。門曰，見說尚書看法華經，是否。曰是。門曰，經中道一切治生產業皆與實相不相違背，且道非非想天有幾人退位。書無語。門曰，尚書且莫艸艸。三經五論師僧，拋卻特入叢林。十年二十年，尚不奈何。尚書又爭得會。書禮拜曰，某甲罪過。

CHAN MASTER MIAOZONG

The master is used to battle and has no need to fast from grains;
Seizing the drum, grabbing the banners, his strength is matchless.
The tiger flies and the dragon prances: who can tell them apart?
Remember: humanity and righteousness triumph over brute strength.

作家慣戰不齋糧
奪鼓攙旗勢莫當
虎驟龍驤誰辦的
反思仁義勝剛強

---

152. The *Lotus Sūtra* notes that when the Buddha began to preach this particular sūtra, five thousand monks and nuns who thought they had already attained nirvana got up and left.
153. This episode can be found in Yuanwu's commentary to case 33 of the *Blue Cliff Record*.

CHAN MASTER BAOCHI

Transfer the generals, hide the troops; how many military forays?
In vain does the Grand Secretary wage a battle of the mouth.
Three thousand swordsmen—where are they now?
All he got was a mournful wind moving across the land.

調將埋兵幾戰征
尚書空使口頭爭
三千劍客今何在
贏得悲風動地生

CHAN MASTER ZUKUI

From inside his sleeve, a face-shattering golden mallet:
Spinning right, turning left, he rides the wind and thunder.
Although so splendid, because he slandered this sūtra,
He immediately left, covered with fur and sprouting horns.

袖裏金鎚劈面來
左旋右轉趁風雷
韶陽因謗斯經故
直得披毛戴角回

CASE 41
Fayan's Fish-Drum

When Fayan[154] heard the fish-drum announcing the meal, he asked a monk if he still heard something. "If just now you heard something, then now you do not. If now you hear something, just now you didn't hear anything."

法眼聞齋魚問僧還聞麼，適來若聞，如今不聞，如今若聞，適來不聞。

CHAN MASTER MIAOZONG

The ear listens as if it were deaf;
The mouth speaks as though mute.
At the tip of Fayan's tongue:
What is real, and what is fake?

耳聽如聾
口說如啞
法眼舌頭
孰真孰假

CHAN MASTER BAOCHI

From the void he plucks a flower;
In the water, he floats the moon.
The crime that has filled universe:
How can one explain it in words?

154. Fayan Wenyi (885–958).

空裏採花
水中漉月
罪兮彌天
焉可分說

CHAN MASTER ZUKUI

A patch of empty substance beyond saying and feeling:
Who has ever explained the realization of the Unborn?
Summon back the shapes and sounds to the dreams in your head;
Roam the timeless-time of the bodhisattva Wonderful Sound.[155]

一片虛凝絕謂情
阿誰曾說悟無生
喚回聲色頭邊夢
直出威音劫外行

155. See note 26.

CASE 42
Fried Sesame Cakes

In the past there was a great master who one day did not go to the hall [for his noontime meal]. When his attendant requested that he go to the hall, he said, "Today I was in the village eating my fill of fried sesame cakes." The attendant said, "Master, you have not even gone in and out of the monastery once today." The master said, "Go ask the head of the village." The attendant had no sooner gone out of the gate when he saw the head of the village coming to thank the master for going to the village to eat fried sesame cakes.

昔有古德，一日不赴堂。侍者請赴堂，德曰，我今日在庄上喫油餈飽者。曰和尚不曾出入。德曰，汝去問庄主者。方出門，忽見庄主歸謝和尚到庄喫油餈。

CHAN MASTER MIAOZONG

Having eaten fried cakes, he does not go to the donor's meal;
The village head comes especially to thank the master.
Seeking, he wanders a thousand mountains, ten thousand streams;
His grass sandals are worn through, but his eyes are still not open.

喫了油餈不赴齋
庄師特特謝師來
千山萬水俱尋遍
踏破芒鞋眼未開

CHAN MASTER BAOCHI

Don't talk of multiplying the body and filling the cosmos;[156]
Inside what family stove has there been fire without smoke?
The level void has been palmed off to the guest from the village,
Revealing a method-gate that is worth quite a lot of money!

謾說分身滿大千
誰家灶裏火無煙
平空脫賺庄家客
露出機關值甚錢

CHAN MASTER ZUKUI

Swallowing three of them, five of them;
Spitting out seven of them, eight of them.
All you need is the attendant to start driveling
Ignoring the words the village-master lets fall.

吞卻三箇五箇
吐卻七箇八箇
秖要侍者流涎
不顧庄師話墮

---

156. Multiplying one's body (*fenshen* 分身) is one of the miraculous capabilities of the Buddha and other enlightened beings.

CASE 43
Dahui Holds Up a Bamboo Whisk

In Dahui's hall, the master held up a bamboo whisk and asked his students, "If you call it a bamboo whisk, that is an affront [to its conditioned existence]; if you don't call it a whisk, you are denying its material reality. You cannot use words, and you cannot not use words."[157]

大慧室中舉竹篦子問學者，喚作竹篦則觸，不喚作竹篦則背，不得有語不得無語。

CHAN MASTER MIAOZONG

Yunmen lifted up his bamboo whisk,
Sages and mortals alike hid away their traces.
When outside of the diamond door, he glowered;
Inside the stable, the wooden horse's face turned red.[158]

雲門舉起竹篦
凡聖潛蹤匿跡
金剛門外生瞋
木馬廄中面赤

157. This kōan centers on Dahui Zonggao, Miaozong's teacher. There are several occasions in his discourse records where he plays with the notion of the whisk, as did his predecessor, the great Tang master Mazu. See for example, *Chan Master Dahui Pujue's Discourse Records* (*Dahui Pujue chanshi yulu*, 大慧普覺禪師法語) T47, 1998A: 825c24–26.

158. The image of the neighing horse appears in a number of Chan dialogues featuring Yunmen. An example found in the *Jingde Transmission of the Lamp* has a monk asking Yunmen, "What is the neighing of the wooden horse of Yunmen?" to which the master replies, "Mountains and rivers are running." (See Chang, *Original Teachings of Ch'an Buddhism*, 293.) However, here Miaozong has given the image an original twist: when combined with the previous line, there is a suggestion of the close interdependence of all things, such that a surge of anger in one place may give rise to a red face in another.

CHAN MASTER BAOCHI

Yunmen's bamboo whisk tips over the pile of poisonous herbs.
Whether turning against it or touching it,
In neither case will it make a great fire!
It completely blocks up the throat and turns over the body;
Why do you need to play with this idler's toy?

Yunmen's bamboo whisk tips over the pile of poisonous herbs.
Whether turning against it or touching it,
In neither case will it make a great fire!
It completely blocks up the throat; how can one breathe out?
Once you've seen through it all you can return;
It is all just a bunch of crap!

雲門竹篦反增藥
忌背兮觸兮成大火
聚塞殺咽喉轉過身
何須弄此閒家具

雲門竹篦去卻藥忌
背觸俱非成大火聚
塞殺咽喉何處出氣
勘破歸來直甚屎屁

CHAN MASTER ZUKUI

Frosted flowers three feet long overwhelm people with their chill;
Buddhas and patriarchs find it difficult to look with the true eye.
If you do not go against the sharp point, you can raise the command,
And the divine radiance will then melt away the skeletal chill.

Be watchful and careful with respect to that which you haven't seen;
Be fearful and afraid with respect to that which you haven't heard.

Before the incipient has taken shape, the brain splits open;
How can one bear to bring up all of this utter confusion?

霜華三尺逼人寒
佛祖難將正眼看
不犯鋒鋩能舉令
神光銷爍髑髏寒

戒慎乎其所不睹
恐懼乎其所不聞
朕兆未形頭腦裂
那堪舉起漫紛紜

Acknowledgments

This book has been some time in the making, and there have been so many friends, family members, and colleagues along the way who have provided much-needed encouragement and support as well as invaluable scholarly assistance. The person to whom I owe the greatest debt of appreciation is Miriam Levering, who helped in so many ways with many of the knotty problems of translation, and whose path-breaking work on Song dynasty Chan Buddhism, and in particular the female Chan master Miaozong and her teacher Dahui Zonggao, has been a constant source of inspiration, information, and insight. I am also very grateful to Wilt L. Idema, who most generously gave of his time and expertise to read over some of the earlier drafts of this translation and offer useful and always-pertinent criticisms and suggestions. And last but by no means least, I must express my deepest and most sincere gratitude to David Kittelstrom and Laura Cunningham of Wisdom Publications, the former for his patience with my dithering and delays, and the latter for her wonderfully meticulous copyediting. Needless to say, all remaining errors, infelicities, or omissions are mine and mine alone. I imagine most translators feel that, with more time and effort, they might have done a more satisfactory job. But at some point, one has to let go and hope that others will benefit from the fruits of one's labors, however imperfect they may be.

Abbreviations

J   *Mingban Jiaxing dazangjing: Jingshan zangban,* 明版嘉興大藏經 ： 徑
山藏版. 40 vols. Taibei: Xinwenfeng chubanshe, 1987.

T   *Taishō shinshū daizōkyō,* 大正新脩大藏經 (Buddhist Canon Newly
Compiled in the Taishō Era). 85 vols. Edited by Takakusu Junjirō and
Watanabe Kaigyoku. 1924–32. Tokyo: Taishō issaikyō kankōkai.

X   *Dainippon zokuzōkyo,* 大日本續藏經 (Great Japanese [Republication
of the] Supplement to the Chinese Buddhist Canon). 150 vols. Edited
by Maeda Eun and Nakano Tatsue. 1905–1912. Kyoto: Zōkyō shoin.
In following the conventions of the CBETA, I use X rather than Z.

Digitized versions of the above three canonical collections are included
in the Chinese Electronic Tripitaka Collections (CBETA) prepared by the
Chinese Buddhist Text Association. Taipei: Zhonghua dianzi fodian xie-
hui, 2015. All citations in this book are to the CBETA online versions.

Bibliography

App, Urs. *Master Yunmen: From the Record of the Chan Master "Gate of the Clouds."* New York: Kodansha International, 1994.

Buswell, Robert. "The 'Short-cut' Approach of K'an-hua Meditation: The Evolution of a Practical Subitism in Chinese Ch'an Buddhism." In *Sudden and Gradual: Approaches to Enlightenment in Chinese Thought*, edited by Peter N. Gregory, 321–377. Honolulu: University of Hawai'i Press, 1987.

Blum, Mark L., trans. *The Nirvana Sutra (Mahāparanirvāna-Sūtra).* Volume 1 (Taishô Volume 12, Number 374). BDK English Tripitaka Series. Berkeley, CA: Bukkyo Dendo Kyokai America, Inc., 2013.

Carter, John Ross and Mahinda Palihawadana, trans. *Dhammapada: The Sayings of the Buddha.* Oxford and New York: Oxford University Press, 2000.

Chang Chung-yuan. *Original Teachings of Chan Buddhism.* Pantheon, 1995.

Cleary, Thomas, trans. *The Blue Cliff Record.* Boston: Shambhala Publications, 2005.

Egan, Charles, trans. *Clouds Thick, Whereabouts Unknown: Poems by Zen Monks of China.* New York: Columbia University Press, 2010.

Ferguson, Andy. *Zen's Chinese Heritage: The Masters and Their Teachings.* 2nd ed. Boston: Wisdom Publications, 2011.

Grant, Beata. *Eminent Nuns: Women Chan Masters of Seventeenth Century China.* Honolulu: University of Hawai'i Press, 2009.

Heine, Steven. *Shifting Shape, Shaping Text: Philosophy and Folklore in the Fox Kōan.* Honolulu: University of Hawai'i Press, 1999.

Hsieh Ding-hwa. "Poetry and Chan 'Gong'an': From Xuedou Chongxian (980–1052) to Wumen Huikai (1183–1260)." *Journal of Song-Yuan Studies* 40 (2010): 39–70.

Hsieh, Evelyn Ding-hwa. "Buddhist Nuns in Sung China." *Journal of Sung-Yuan Studies* 30 (2000): 63–96.

Kirchner, Thomas Yūhō. *Entangling Vines: A Classic Collection of Zen Kōans.* Boston: Wisdom Publications, 2013.

Levering, Miriam. "Dahui Zonggao (1089–1163): The Image Created by His Stories about Himself and by His Teaching Style." In *Zen Masters*, edited by Steven Heine and Dale Wright, 91–116. Oxford and New York: Oxford University Press, 2010.

———. "A Monk's Literary Education: Dahui's Friendship with Juefan Hui-hong." *Chung-Hwa Buddhist Journal* 13.2 (2000): 369–384.

———. "Women Ch'an Masters: The Teacher Miao-tsung as Saint." In *Women Saints in World Religions*, edited by Arvind Sharma. Albany: State University of New York Press, 2000.

———, trans. "The Biography of Miaozong," In *Zen Sourcebook: Traditional Documents from China, Korea, and Japan*, edited by Stephen Addiss with Stanley Lombardo and Judith Roitman. Indianapolis/Cambridge: Hackett Publishing Company, 2008.

Lynn, Richard, trans. *The Classic of Changes: A New Translation of the I Ching as Interpreted by Wang Bi.* New York: Columbia University Press, 1994.

Strong, John. *Relics of the Buddha.* Motilal Banarsidass, 2007.

Watson, Burton, trans. *The Zen Teachings of Master Lin-Chi.* New York: Columbia University Press, 1999.

Watson, Burton, trans. *The Complete Works of Zhuangzi.* New York: Columbia University Press, 2013.

Welter, Albert. *Monks, Rulers, and Literati: The Political Ascendancy of Chan Buddhism.* New York: Oxford University Press, 2006.

Wu, Jiang. *Enlightenment in Dispute: The Reinvention of Chan Buddhism in Seventeenth-Century China.* New York and Oxford: Oxford University Press, 2011.

Index

About the Translator

BEATA GRANT is professor of Chinese and religious studies in the Department of East Asian Languages and Cultures at Washington University in St. Louis. She is the author of *Daughters of Emptiness: Poems of Chinese Buddhist Nuns*; *Eminent Nuns: Women Chan Masters of Seventeenth-Century China*; and, with Wilt L. Idema, *The Red Brush: Writing Women of Imperial China* and *Escape from Blood Pond Hell: The Tales of Mulian and Woman Huang*. She is a native of New Mexico and lives in St. Louis, Missouri.

Also Available from Wisdom Publications

Daughters of Emptiness
Poems of Chinese Buddhist Nuns
Beata Grant

"This beautiful book testifies to the power of Buddhist practice to nourish the human spirit even when war, physical hardship, class discrimination, and oppression seem insurmountable."
—*Turning Wheel*

The Hidden Lamp
Stories from Twenty-Five Centuries of Awakened Women
Zenshin Florence Caplow and Reigetsu Susan Moon
Foreword by Zoketsu Norman Fischer

"An amazing collection. This book gives the wonderful feel of the sincerity, the great range, and the nobility of the spiritual work that women are doing and have been doing, unacknowledged, for a very long time. An essential and delightful book."
—John Tarrant, author of *The Light Inside the Dark*

Zen Women
Beyond Tea Ladies, Iron Maidens, and Macho Masters
Grace Schireson
Foreword by Miriam Levering

"An exceptional and powerful classic with great depth, humor, and clarity."
—Joan Halifax, abbess of Upaya Zen Center

Entangling Vines
A Classic Collection of Zen Koans
Thomas Yuhō Kirchner
Foreword by Nelson Foster

"A masterpiece. It will be our inspiration for 10,000 years."
—Robert Aitken, author of *Taking the Path of Zen*

The Clouds Should Know Me by Now
Buddhist Poet Monks of China
Edited by Mike O'Connor and Red Pine
Introduced by Andrew Schelling

"Here is a breathtaking millennium of Buddhist poet-monks."
—*Inquiring Mind*

Awesome Nightfall
The Life, Times, and Poetry of Saigyō
William LaFleur

"Saigyō's poems are masterful mind-language challenges. Bill LaFleur's deeply understanding translations present us with the snake-like energy of the syntax, and the illuminated world that was called out by one man's lifetime of walking and meditation is again right here."
—Gary Snyder

About Wisdom Publications

Wisdom Publications is the leading publisher of classic and contemporary Buddhist books and practical works on mindfulness. To learn more about us or to explore our other books, please visit our website at wisdompubs.org or contact us at the address below.

Wisdom Publications
199 Elm Street
Somerville, MA 02144 USA

We are a 501(c)(3) organization, and donations in support of our mission are tax deductible.

Wisdom Publications is affiliated with the Foundation for the Preservation of the Mahayana Tradition (FPMT).